Stephen Hassum.

12, 7, 75,

Small Garden Design

Small
Garden Design

Michael Jefferson-Brown

Illustrated by R. Theobald

JOHN GIFFORD LTD. · LONDON W.C.2.

SBN 70710221 9

Published in Great Britain by
John Gifford Ltd., London.
Printed by Compton Printing Ltd.,
London and Aylesbury.

Contents

Introduction

The Garden of Eden being spacious, well designed and planted with mature trees and plants was perfect. Adam could find nothing to do, or almost nothing. For the fallen sons of Adam in the 20th century the garden may provide just the right amount of pleasurable work, or it may provide more work than is wanted and the hundred and one decisions that endanger happy mental and emotional equilibrium like the poor civil servant sorting potatoes for the farmer. The ReadyMix lorry backs its load and there goes another bit of England.

Collectors of match-boxes get much enjoyment from their spare-time occupation but they have still a long way to go before the fascination of their pastime reaches the level of what is the number one hobby, gardening. The spinach sits sadly on the small child's plate, the child eats it to do good to itself and perhaps the taste for spinach is formed. So must the taste for gardening be formed in many cases, but each year more gardens are created, more people take up the hobby, more discernment is exercised, and more interest is shown in Mr. Smith's small lot by Big Brother I.C.I. and other organizations interested in the growing market created by gardeners. Plastic gnome salesmen will be knocking at the door any minute now.

One major factor distinguishes the trend of gardening today

from the gardening of the past. The proportion of small to large gardens is growing and the size of the small garden is diminishing. It may not be altogether a bad thing, as probably more pleasure is gained from a small garden kept in good order comfortably, and planted carefully with worthwhile plants, than in trying to maintain some form of civilization over a larger empire where rebellious weeds continue to rise against a thinly stretched gardener encouraged or instructed by well meaning advice from the marriage partner. A canvas is to be painted, not a mural round the walls of Princetown jail.

The smaller the painting, the bigger the smudge. The smaller the garden the more important that it should be well designed, the more important it is to make the most of its best natural features and minimize its worst ones. And I certainly do not think one should be afraid of words like design and planning, for I take these to mean basically commonsense applied to problems that have been carefully thought about and closely observed. I shall not deal in absolutes, which is as well in a century in which absolutes in aesthetic judgements have vanished from the scene and pop singers are worshipped like gods.

'But,' said the dwarf, 'what do you mean by small?' It is of course, I reply, a relative thing, a sort of as-long-as-a-piece-of string definition. I mean the sort of garden plot seen around a house on a modern estate, probably not so much bigger than twice the area covered by bricks and mortar in house and garage. But I imagine that what we think about may be applicable to gardens up to the size of $\frac{1}{4}$ acre or slightly more.

'I know my job,' said the Bearded Lady, 'What are your qualifications?' Of course, I know it often happens that the author feels obliged to excuse another book, or would like to jot down some of his life history to show why he is uniquely fit to write the monumental treatise offered with due show of modesty. Being a nurseryman is hardly a recommendation, for a nurseryman's garden can often rival the farmer's garden. But having moved house several times, I have had the opportunity of making several gardens and plenty of mistakes. This book merely tries to explore some of the problems of the small garden and make some suggestions, but it does recognize that the small garden poses problems of their own and that we may have to do some fresh thinking.

Square One

Of course Cromwell is the cause of the English suburban garden. He lurks behind every privet hedge. Unconsciously the gardener is powered by the great puritan urge to find work for idle hands. He reaches for the spade or the secateurs. Wilkinson's sword flashes through the floribundas. The Frenchman sits in his cafe, the German quoffs in the beer-garden, the Swede takes the boat out, the Italian, well I'm not too sure what the Italian is about but I'm pretty sure it's got little to do with King Alfred, Ena Harkness, or the latest incurve sport. English life is real and gardening is very earnest. Long live the Royal Horticultural Society, the Lord's Day Observance Society, and Greenfingers of the Daily X.

Let us attempt a little seriousness and examine our terms of reference a little more closely. 'Small Garden Design.' 'Small' we have measured in the introduction, and similarly 'design' we have hazarded a working definition for, and this leaves only the word 'garden'.

Can we define 'garden'. It is a created thing; it may copy nature closely or it may not, and in that garden closest to nature some artificial restraint or balance has been created or maintained. Where even the lightest hand has created there is present a sense of purpose, and here is the main question we can ask in defining what we mean by garden. Why do we create a garden? Approached from another path we can ask, why do we garden?

There is no one answer. Each person has a different purpose or set of purposes. The reasons may vary from the exceptional council tenant, who keeps the garden tidy to prevent eviction or a form of fine, to the other gardener who sees his garden as a living work of art.

The parents with young children see the plot as a playing ground, some see it as an outside room complete with barbeque, others as means to provide the table with the fresh fruits and vegetables with the tastes that the bought article seems to lack, the retired couple view the garden as a peaceful haven providing interest, beauty and contentment. And as the viewpoint changes so the form of the garden must change. The retired couple do not want to undertake the navvying that the enthusiastic exhibitor of show vegetables is willing to undertake. The bowling green lawn that suits one garden will not suit the parent of a budding Hutton or Bradman.

Jeeves would be ready to point out that the creation of a suitable garden for a certain person depends on 'the psychology of the individual.' Lord Emsworth's admirable work for maintaining the highest standards of the traditional stately home garden is not completed without a clash of temperaments with the gardener McAlister. The moss below the Yew Avenue must be maintained, though McAlister would like some clean tarmac.

GARDEN DESIGN

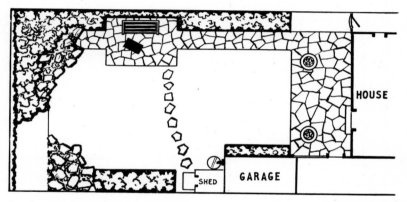

In the garden of one person the emphasis will be on display, an extrovert pageant of colour contrived to last as long as possible through the year, salvias are commanded in hundreds, squads of geraniums don guardsmen's tunics, dahlias dazzle in primary and secondary colours. But over the fence the accent is on the rare plant, a fine Witch Hazel lights up a corner in winter, a group of Asiastic primulas flourish in a moist spot, and plants with no common English names grow and are tended with lavish care

5

that the plantsman gives who sees first the individual plant and only hazily recognizes the overall need for a garden plan.

There is always work in a garden, even the most labour saving one. Very few would have it otherwise providing the work is in a sensible ratio to the results and enjoyment. A garden is a changing thing, it varies with the seasons and may mature with age or undergo several transitions. Normally in suggesting a design the ideas will embrace both some ideal of perfection

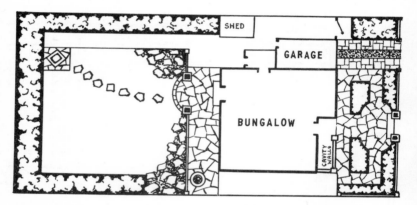

to be gained after some years as well as the immediate effect. The design is not a fixed but a continuing and developing one. So even while the younger parent is coping with the need for playing space for lusty infants, he may spare thought for the future main features of the garden which will come into their own when the teenagers have gone off demonstrating or hitch hiking in Africa. He plants the Cherry Trees or the Apple species that will spread branches over the former Wembley turf.

Chapter 1

The House and the Garden

A small garden is normally going to be dominated by the house and garage built on it. To a lesser degree it may be overlooked by other houses. We can allow a greater or a lesser amount of the formal feeling of the buildings to permeate the garden design. The buildings can be further emphasised by simple or even stark design in the garden around, or the house and garden may begin to merge together. Shrubs may grow on the house walls, a paved area near the house may have on it tubs with shrubs and flowering plants so that there is produced the feeling of a garden-room, neither all garden or all house. On the character of the house much of the rest of the design will follow. The simplicity of a georgian house is probably best enjoyed if it appears to have been built from a platform, possibly a paved platform with low balustrading or low formal walls marking the boundary of the platform and from here on the garden proper may begin. On the other hand a timbered house or cottage seems to belong to the ground and to have grown from it, and it seems in keeping for the garden to approach to the very windows and-walls.

The new brick-built house tends to favour the more formal approach to design. Red bricks make a pleasing background for the green of some of the less hardy evergreen shrubs such as the winter flowering *Garrya elliptica*. To my mind the climbing roses look more at home on the walls of older property or growing up pillars or trunks away from the walls of new houses. But it often seems a mistake to try to crowd the walls of a new house with the plants that look more at home on a cottage, pink roses and honeysuckle belong to the cottage, though with some of the new lasting well-produced trellis supports many plants can be encouraged to grow up modern walls with good effect. The evergreens are often the most pleasing, both for the fact that they do not undress for the winter and for the permanent feeling and green contrast for the normal red brickwork.

The house dominates the garden, but it is the eyes of the householder that are the most important. We must view the property from the roadside and approach but we must consider any design also from the windows of the house. With the popularity of the large picture window, we might consider the garden in terms of a picture. We would expect a more or less unimpeded foreground, with our eyes taken deeper into the picture by the lines of paths, of lawns or walls that reach as far into the distance as we can possibly suggest. The picture is balanced with a group of shrubs here to one side and the summer house half submerged by creepers further back on the other side. The path curves behind that group of shrubs towards something suggested. The path curving out of view is the most intriguing of features. It may only lead to the incinerator but from the house window it can be more exciting and satisfying than a straight path that ends with the full stop of the back garden fence.

More often neglected is the variety and satisfaction to be

(Top) A heather garden in Surrey

(Bottom) An informal flagstone arrangement for a cottage garden

Hostas bordering flagstone steps

Ornamental stonework and wrought iron work makes a welcome change

Water garden

gained by the varying of heights in the garden. Even a few inches up or down literally give added dimension to the garden design. How much more effective the herbaceous border that is of sensible width and is built up at the back perhaps a foot over the height at the front thus giving added stature to the plants at the back. It varies the soil conditions by providing sharper surface drainage at the back and cooler rootruns at the front thus enabling the knowing gardener to plant a much wider range of plants.

The provision of a built-up bed or beds should be well considered for, not only may they give added height, depth and richness to the design masses, but they can provide the homes for plants that would otherwise be difficult to accommodate. Soil conditions in raised beds can be made to the plant-customer's requirements. Certainly these raised beds are a boon to the more elderly or less active gardener who can enjoy focusing his eyes on plants within easy range and can tend them without the discomfort of bending or kneeling.

This consideration of heights, the verticals in design as well as the horizontals, may lead us to consider the garden in another aspect. We started by likening it to a picture, we could perhaps have suggested that it was a stage and that we might employ some of the stages legitimate subterfuges. Down the wings of our stage viewed from the house windows we may expect to see two uncompromising fences. We can consider clothing these with rambler roses and other plants, but we could tackle the problem another way. We might build a number of walls at right angles to the boundary like short curtains screening the wings, coming a few feet into the garden and so breaking our view of the fence and also creating the exciting possibilities of alcoves that we can design separately to use or to plant with varying combinations of plants. Perhaps we may have alcoves devoted to different times of the year, perhaps devoted to special foliage effects, the grey alcove, the red alcove, etc. Or perhaps the alcoves could be designed to take special care of particular classes of plants ranging from the lime lovers, to those that exist on almost nothing but peat.

The range of decorative screening bricks which allow light and air through are the obvious kind to use for this purpose, for they are attractive alone and melt into the garden scene well. Indeed the hollow patterning of these walls does make the most of both the upward dimension and the depth of such a wall.

Similar interior screening effects can be obtained with metal railings or open wood railings. Certainly some very attractive garden effects can be gained by allowing plants like *Cotoneaster horizontalis* to grow up and through upright railings. The interplay of the rigidly upright lines of the rails with the fishbone patterning of the Cotoneaster can be most exciting.

Persuing the question of the varying heights in the garden, a point should be made of the value of this device in design for providing the bold line or feature to bring to life what might otherwise be a somewhat ordinary garden. Where the height varies a low containing-wall may be built with perhaps a step or two. Where we introduce steps we have the opportunity of creating a very pleasing feature either incorporating plants or not. The steps again emphasize a direction and lead the eye into the picture. Steps may be needed close to the house and can be very effective here, perhaps leading from the paved platform area close to the house into the garden proper. But steps in the middle distance, say two-thirds the way down the garden, can

THE GARDEN SHOULD BE VIEWED FROM THE WINDOW

give that pleasurable feeling of intriguing direction and make one wonder what lies beyond. Often this feeling is something not consciously thought but is nevertheless present.

Naturally the designing in heights and depths will usually

11

depend most heavily on the use of plants, especially the shrubs and trees. In the restricted space of the small garden good use can be made of the pointed conical trees such as the many pleasant conifers of the *C. lawsoniana* brotherhood or of such smaller but striking trees like the flowering cherry, *Prunus hillierii* 'Spire.'

We do not have to stop at soil level when thinking of the verticals in our design. The conifer like an arrow takes our eye up, but put a mirror at its base and we look down into mysterious depths. Even quite a small area of water can do this most attractively and effectively. Water of course adds a great deal to any garden. A stream of moving water splashing over rocks and busily bubbling its way through the waterside plants gives the garden movement and a special livliness that nothing else can achieve. With the apparatus now available this need not be an idle pipedream, but of course in a small garden it will always be easier to provide the still mirror water of a small formal or informal pond. Now that there are so many ready-made pool liners the most critical work has been taken out of pool making.

A pool of water mirrors its surrounds, the tall trunks reach down into mysterious depths, into the water where life began. But we would not surround our small pond with trees, we want to see some sky mirrored there. Around we want to see the patterns cut into space by the exciting water-loving Gunneras, the swords of water irises, the gorgeous double golden marsh marigolds, the trollius's globes, and the splendid candelabra of primulas.

We look from our windows over the paved area by the house,

across the green lawn by the path to the small pool, and then beyond the pool up steps to that turning path. Now from the turning path we look back at the house and we note the walls that cry out for scrambling plants from far distant lands to cover them. We note the path and realize how vital it is in this blessed climate of ours. We clothe the walls in the next chapter, here we consider the paths.

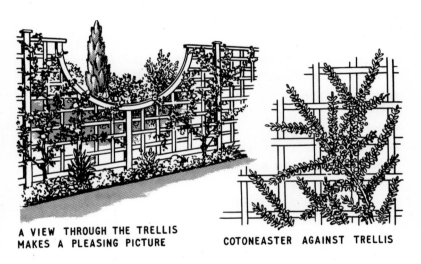

A VIEW THROUGH THE TRELLIS MAKES A PLEASING PICTURE

COTONEASTER AGAINST TRELLIS

Paths

It is of course the first problem and duty of the gardener to see to his lines of communication. On the virgin building site civilization follows the postman from front gate to front door, the house-wife from kitchen to dustbin, and head of the household from armchair to the incinerator at the bottom of the garden. The

13

paths, together with the walls and fences, form the basic framework of the garden design, the skeleton around which everything else should grow. The first function of a path is that it should be of use at all times in all weathers and should be durable. The second function is that it should look well. If the two things can be married we have a successful bit of work under our feet.

As soon as definite suggestions are made there are going to be objections from some, for what suits one place may not suit another and what expense can be justified by one may be thought undue extravagance by another. I am going to put down what I feel about the various types of paths and risk being pedantic, and risk being thought misguided.

Gravel paths

A wide path of clean washed gravel neatly contained at the edges can look most agreeable. The colour is warm and pleasing, usually supplied in a variety of colours mixed so that the mosaic effect is predominately a rich sandy colour. The objections to the gravel path are several. First, as the gravel moves, the more the path is used by vehicles or people walking, the more the gravel is going to be displaced and require raking true again. Secondly, however clean the original gravel was, it is inevitable that there will be a build up of detritus that will encourage the growth of grass, moss, and weeds which will then require killing by poison, flame gun or by being plucked out. Much can be done to provide a weedfree base on which to place the gravel, but the path is never going to be weed proof.

14

GARDEN PATHS

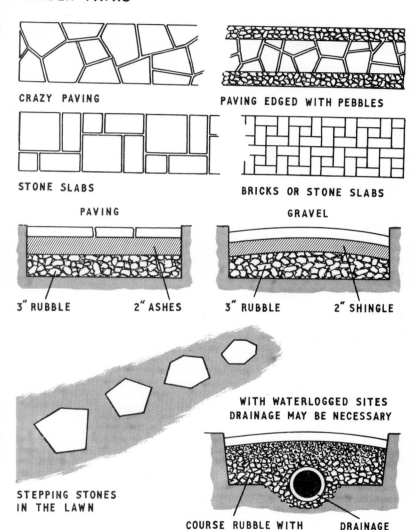

CRAZY PAVING

PAVING EDGED WITH PEBBLES

STONE SLABS

BRICKS OR STONE SLABS

PAVING

GRAVEL

3" RUBBLE   2" ASHES

3" RUBBLE   2" SHINGLE

STEPPING STONES
IN THE LAWN

WITH WATERLOGGED SITES
DRAINAGE MAY BE NECESSARY

COURSE RUBBLE WITH
SAND OR CLINKER

DRAINAGE
PIPES

Where small children abound, the temptation is ever present to use the gravel for harmlessly filling buckets and tipping them on the lawn or more beligerently exploring their ballistic worthiness. For main paths I rate the gravel path lowly, a relic of past ages when John would touch his forelock and sweep the pebbles into place again. This is not to say I would not like to use gravel for its decorative value elsewhere, perhaps an oblong enclosed alongside a formal pool may look well.

Ash paths
I have seen many paths made up out of weathered ash that served well and looked neat, but they were usually in the kitchen gardens of larger gardens. Well contained, with their level above the surrounding soil, and maintained in a weed free condition, the ash path can look neat. But in the small garden it is unlikely to be of much use. Nor is it weed free.

Tarmac paths
Is there a place for tarmac in the garden? The question can be answered both ways. Where cars may enter and where they may stand, tarmac is most serviceable and of course does not show the discoloration that the dropping of oil can show on other surfaces. But if it is to be done it is best done well. Nothing is more annoying than to find perennial weeds growing up through tarmac, nor does it bring joy to the beholder when edges begin to crumble and the boundary of tarmaced area and garden begins to be a disputed line. The foundations of tarmac should be good with a fall allowed for surface drainage. Any

weed root left below the foundations should be most thoroughly poisoned. The edges of the tarmaced area should be bounded with concrete curb stones or in some similar thorough manner. The objections to tarmacs other than those mentioned are that it is flavoured slightly by its public utility image. Also the black colour may not be as an attractive a colour as could otherwise be managed.

Concrete paths

Concrete paths properly made are extremely durable and although perhaps somewhat harsh in appearance this can be ameliorated by using a colouring agent to make the concrete a buff or pinkish shade. Like many other types of path this type can be changed from an adequate one to an impressive one by the use of good edgings. The narrow concrete curbs allowed to stand a couple or so inches proud of the edge of the paths gives the whole thing the same finished appearance as a picture gets when it is framed. Naturally the curbs should be well set in concrete so that they remain fixed and true, and the curbs every now and again will allow nearly an inch gap to let rainwater drain away.

Brick paths

The look of a brick path with the bricks set narrow edge upwards and in herring-bone or jogjag pattern can be most attractive. There is a lot of work in such a path for if it is to be attempted it must be done well and I believe it is best to set the bricks on concrete and to point them. A brick path can be a disaster if it

17

is allowed to get weed ridden. The bricks used in such a path must be good quality ones not liable to break and crumble after frost or with wear.

Paved paths

For all main paths I believe that the most serviceable and possibly the most attractive are to be made from manufactured paving stones. Some of the larger sizes, though very good once in place, are heavy to manoeuvre. The 3 by 2-feet slabs 2 inches thick are heavy to move. The square 2 by 2-foot ones are very much easier to use though it may be thought that the square shape is perhaps less pleasing. I use these 2 by 2-foot slabs and, though the majority are the normal neutral shade, we do add a sprinkling of red and buff ones to avoid the dead look of all grey. The red ones seem to be the most useful contrast to the grey, they fade less than the buffs usually. There are, of course, several different types of slabs manufactured, some firms specializing in a more decorative approach and offering various sizes to be used together to give a much more varied effect than that obtained from the laying of one standard size.

I buy our slabs ready-made and I believe most would find this the easiest way, but sometimes it can be difficult to get delivery of small numbers of slabs and then the handyman may wish to make his own. This is no very difficult task. Slabs should certainly be $1\frac{1}{4}$ inches thick and would be much better at 2 inches. Any piece of level ground can be used to work on. Wooden edges to the thickness decided on can border the ground, 6 feet apart perhaps where a series of three 2-foot square slabs are going to be made. Over the base of the ground will have been laid half an inch of coarse sand. This makes it easier to lift the slabs and leaves them with a rough sandy texture below. For every square yard of 2-inch thick slabs to be constructed you will need about 48 lb of cement, and amounts of sand and aggregate graded to about $\frac{1}{2}$ inch in equal proportion to each other and totalling a little over one and a half cubic feet. In the form of buckets this would be one bucket of cement to one and a half each of sand and aggregate. For every four bucketfuls of this mixture one would use half a bucket of water, assuming the sand to be damp and not sodden. After the concrete has been thoroughly mixed and laid, it may be left for an hour or two and then cut with a straight edge and trowel to the sizes required. Naturally the concrete should be cut its complete thickness. During the four or five days hardening they should be kept just damp with sacking or other similar covering. The slabs can then be lifted with a spade and stored on edge ready for use. There are colouring matters that can be added to the concrete when mixing to relieve the possible drabness of the natural grey. We find a red colouring gives a warm appearance, though we only use occasional coloured ones amongst the grey and would hesitate to use all coloured ones.

Where permanent paved areas are to be constructed one can perhaps use some of the most pleasing effects possible with cobbles or bricks let into a concrete base. One can buy concrete slabs with round cobbles stones already let into them and most pleasing they look. The textured effects to be gained by such means can look attractive at all times.

Having laid the paths, the trading routes of our empire, we can start to look at some of the problems and challenges that confront us.

Chapter 2

We've all got Problems

There is the weather, and the government, and that black cat, and some more things that we do not seem to be able to do much about. It is a matter of challenge and response, said some-one. 'It is a matter,' said the dwarf to the giant, 'of whether you are going to get off my foot.' It is probably a matter of whether the Almighty has given us a sense of humour and the ability to use ingenuity to overcome our problems. 'Come back Guy Fawkes, all is forgiven.'

The small garden is likely to have more problems than the larger one. The house is likely to cast a greater proportion in deep shade as are the walls and fences. Drainage may also be a greater problem for the same reason, the bricks and mortar impeding natural drainage. Likewise a gentle breeze can be channelled through houses to form a promising young gale. The very soil from which we create our garden may have been adulterated by the lifting of subsoil by contractors and the incorporating of unrotting builders waste. The soil in a town garden may have been used for so many decades as to have lost its health and life. The only way in which the small garden gains over the larger one is that inch by square inch one must assume the statistical probability of there being fewer weeds.

At the outset, the two basic problems are likely to be the

boundaries of the plot and drainage of the soil. For the first three feet of height at least, the more secure and windproof the boundary the better. A wall is going to be the best and the most expensive. A wall allows very good support for many plants that one could not otherwise so easily grow, it does help keep warm and protected some of the less hardy plants. Wooden fences will be useful in the same way and useful in direct proportion to

WOODEN FENCING

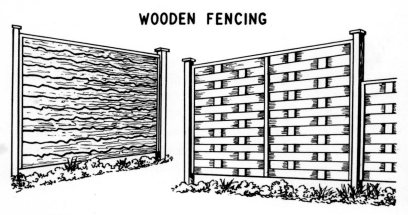

RUSTIC-LAPPED FENCING   **INTERWOVEN FENCING**

their strength. At the bottom of the scale in usefulness is the wire netting barrier that lets all the wind through and of course retains no warmth. If wire netting it is to be, then a hedge of some kind may become a high priority item, assuming that there is no neighbourhood agreement for an overall garden landscape effect.

Hedges we have mentioned in another place so that we shall

not dwell too long on the problem here. What we are creating is a barrier, and a boundary. It may well be that we need not restrict ourselves to one species for the hedge, and that we need not consider it as being a living geometrical wall, but rather as a grouping of shrubby plants that just happen to mark the extent of our territory. Certainly in this way we can combine the attractive foliage colour effect to be got by using conifers, many evergreen shrubs, beeches that clipped retain their rusty dead foliage through the winter, and the denser growing of the deciduous shrubs.

A point should be made here. If a wire-netting fence is to be used, it is well worth getting the plastic covered netting which lasts longer, looks much better, and gives the plants better support in that the temperature of the plastic does not soar as high or get so cold as the metal.

The walls as a garden

Where our horizontal square yards are limited we should certainly look to the walls to provide us with additional acreage of garden. There are many shrubs and plants that will hold or flatten themselves against a wall naturally but there are very many more that we might not think of in this role that can be persuaded to fan their branches more two than three dimensionally. Thus we can curtain the walls with a variety of shrubs and where we want greater floral effect we plant climbers like honeysuckle and clematis which will not damage the appearance of their supporting hosts but which will give us extra foliage and floral beauty.

Those that need support either temporarily or throughout life can be aided in various ways. Some branches may be simply pegged back by a short length of cloth or plastic secured to nails driven into the mortar on each side of the branch. More elaborately one can drive nails into the mortar at one end of the wall and from this nail stretch wire to a nail at the other end. On a long stretch there is need of extra nails along the length, say at six-foot intervals. Several such strands arranged horizontally will make it relatively easy to support most wall plants, but of course the twining ones will need vertical wire if this is to the basis of their support and they are not going to rely on a host shrub or tree. Trellis work may be used and can be effective, especially for the support of shrubs which need help in their younger years, but which harden their backbones later and can stand on their own. Trellis, especially much that is sold at present, is not a long lived item. But not every modern production is a poorer counterpart of its older prototypes. There is a very useful and attractive fan-shaped wall support for an individual shrub produced now which may well be the answer for us.

If we review briefly the plants that we can use to clothe our walls we should start with the independent minded ones which support themselves. We have to start then with the ivies. I am not an ivy hater, being born far enough away from the rather oppressively over-ivied days of Queen Victoria. The wild ivy has many sports and, in any form, this humble plant can still be defended from its detractors. First, we may say that it will live anywhere in sun or shade, in any soil, or any climate. Then we

attractive show of Azaleas in a walled garden

A wooded town garden

may add that it does not shirk its duty in the winter, dropping its leaves and hibernating like the Virginia Creeper. Then it may be pointed out that even the commonest of plants like this can repay the second glance to enjoy its leaf form and colouring.

SCREEN WALLING

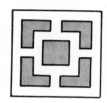

In a shady spot we might use the golden leaved 'Buttercup' to brighten the gloom. Where a lighter dress is wanted we might use the *Hedera helix caenwoodiana* with its small leaves so deeply cut back that the lobes might be claws helping it to

25

climb the wall. For the boldest effect we might bring in an ivy from overseas, *H. colchica*, with its huge dark leaves that are but sketchily lobed and can measure well over six inches across and perhaps ten long.

The Virginia Creeper is such a useful and easy plant, and produces such wonderful autumn colouring, that even the most selective of plantsmen will welcome it in the garden and be happy to sweep up the piles of fallen leaves. This plant is known under many names, most usually nowadays as *Parthenocissus quinquefolia* which sounds more like a disease than a plant to me. This is the plant with the sucker discs that help it to climb almost any surface and has provided a wonderful subject for time-lapse photography when one can watch the growing shoots and the tendrils waving and exploring space till they touch the surface that they clamp on to. The other Virginia Creeper, *P. vitacea,* is perhaps even more brilliant in foliage though it climbs by the support of its twisting tendrils in more common vinelike fashion. It is often used to go up pergolas and along their rafters so that the long growths hang down, forming a living curtain.

There are at least three climbing Hydrangeas, but easily the best is *H. petiolaris*. It is a particularly useful plant for growing on a north wall which it will clothe to almost any height. It grows strongly and has typical hydrangea foliage which is deciduous. The flowers are cream, the flattish bunch being formed of the tiny centre ones and a ring of large sterile ones around the outside. It adheres to the wall just like an ivy. Other species not naturally climbers can be grown up the wall.

Variously coloured forms of *H. serrata* will go up some five or six feet and grow rather wider. White, pink and blue forms of this species have the lace-cap design, the central flowers small and insignificant, the marginal ones being a half to nearly an inch across.

Of the many fine *Cotoneaster* species, the one so commonly used against the wall, *C. horizontalis*, is still probably the best. Even the pattern of its bare branches is attractive. *C. microphylla* with round, small dark-green leaves may be encouraged to send long branches up a wall with some small support, the deluded shrub keeping flat against the wall thinking it is hugging the ground or a rock face. Its pretty pinky-red berries are delightful, a few small twigs making most pleasing table decorations. *C. rotundifolia* may also be persuaded to climb a wall, and here one sees an affinity between this species and *C. horizontallis* with its rather stiffly arranged opposite rows of branches. It is certainly a most prodigous cropper with its fruit left out through the winter often into February or March and with foliage too. It is hardly such a ground hugger as *C. horizontalis* and its berries are somewhat larger.

The *Cotoneasters* lead us naturally enough to the Firethorns, the various *Pyracanthas* whose huge crops of berries gleam from so many suburban walls. *P. coccinea lalandei* with its massive bunches of orange fruits is one often seen, but this has now been rather superseded by new seedling kinds. 'Kazan' is similar but is both stronger growing and hardier, but our choice might well finally fall on *P. coccinea* 'Orange Charmer' and 'Yellow Charmer ,' both most prolific berriers that keep their fruits well into the winter and appear to be more resistant to disease than most other thorns. There may well still be a place for the species *P. atalantioides* with its larger evergreen leaves and its masses of scarlet berries. It will stand full square to the weather facing any point of the compass. True its berries are slightly smaller and ripen rather later but they will often be there in shining colour in March. These firethorns need support in their early years and are best when kept pruned back fairly close to the wall.

Flowers from the winter-blooming *Jasminum nudiflorum* will often open whilst the berries of the firethorns are still bright. This scrambling shrub certainly needs support, unless it is allowed to grow in a place where it can scramble over the ground, probably rooting as it goes and forming a ground cover plant, or even better sending out sweeping fans of green branches over some large rock or down some retaining wall, thus reversing its normal straight-jacketed performance going up the wall. It is of course a shrub that should be in every garden. Its many stems studded with primroses are going to provide an irresistible temptation for the flower arranger starved of flowers in the winter.

Again we must surely take one of the many cydonias up a wall whether we call it this, or japonica or *Chaenomeles*, the current favourite name for a well-loved shrub with red, pink, orange or white flowers. Within reason the harder it is pruned back to the wall the better the shrub flowers, certainly the wood against the wall probably ripens that much better and provides the flower buds more freely.

If we can dispel from our mind the picture of the fantastic 'Lynwood Gold' forsythias and their kin, we might the better appreciate the more gentle beauty of *F. suspensa* as it is taken up a wall and its many flowering branches reaching out and down towards us with their golden rent.

Ceonothus in their many shades of blue and with their dark-

PYRACANTHA · FIRETHORN   CYDONIA · JAPONICA

green foliage will allow themselves to be shaped against a wall, as will the *Escallonias* and *Euonymus* species and hybrids. I think that before I allowed wall room for these, despite their beauty, I should see that we had a place booked for *Garrya elliptica* with its dark evergreen leaves and winter catkins.

Once we have some of the more stalwart species stationed on the wall we might turn our attention to climbers that as auxiliaries will provide extra colour and interest at various times of the year. Thus we may allow clematis, as species like *C. montana* or as large flowered hybrids, to clamber up between shrubs or over and through them. We might allow honeysuckles to do the same. Or we could bring climbers more usually seen growing up and over pillars or pergolas and let them loose on the wall. The Dutchman's Pipe, *Aristolochia sipho* (*A. macrophylla*), might well be one, though we may have to drop this name for all the Dutchmen I know seem to smoke cigars of one shape or another. It is a climber with twisting stems and most handsome large leaves usually variously likened in shape to some internal organ, heart or kidney, but they do vary in shape and in size. They can be from three or four inches to almost a foot long and close on the same width. The apple-green foliage is joined in June by the curiously shaped flowers coloured in tones of yellow and green. We might also think to bring the Passion flower up the wall, for though it is not a really hardy plant it will often survive several years on a sheltered wall, showing itself then to be almost evergreen and holding tight with tendrils. The flowers are both curiously constructed and beautiful and from June till the beginning of October there are usually some to examine and wonder at. Of course a somewhat tender plant like this can be protected by its hardy neighbours.

Soil and drainage

Nothing is more important in a small garden than the drainage of the soil. This is obviously tied up with the texture of the soil itself. The heavier the soil the greater the problem. There has to be a three-pronged attack on the problem. First, we shall probably have to make some form of actual drain. Second, we can vary the levels of parts of the garden to heighten certain borders and have lower levels elsewhere, so that to a certain extent we can plant our garden according to the amount of moisture the soil is likely to contain, or to the sharpness of drainage needed by our various plants. Third, we can help to change the physical constitution of the soil by using chemicals or by incorporating fresh material with the soil with or without evacuating existing soil.

One is unlikely to have a house sited on a bog, so that it is safe to assume that one is not liable to repeated flooding and that the problem is to deal with excess water at certain times after a period of heavy rainfall. If we are fortunate we may be able to take out trenches some eighteen inches deep and lay field drains falling to a lower area or into an existing drain. We may go to the trouble of collecting builders' rubble and other intractible material and, in a large excavation, make a sump drain that will take surplus water. But on the whole, it may most often suffice to see to it that borders are well built-up so that at least a good proportion of the roots of any plant are likely to be growing through a soil which does not remain waterlogged for long. There is some evidence that there is a form of specialization about the function of roots of many plants and that some are likely to deal with greater quantities of soil water than others. Paths can be effectively used as a means of draining the garden if they are built on deep foundations of bricks and rubbish that will act as a drain for the surrounding soil.

In a very small town garden it may be that the soil has been exhausted by years of use and misuse. It could be that quantities of this soil could be replaced by compost bought in from a nursery. Even if such extreme measures are not attempted or are not needed, the incorporating of fresh soil, or leaf mould, or peat can usually have a tonic effect on the life of the soil. The top dressing of such soil as an annual function can have a very great built-up effect. Through the late spring and summer months the use of peat as a mulch will do much to retain moisture in the soil as well as smothering any germinating weed seed.

Weed control is always a problem though in the smaller garden the size of the problem is obviously less. Nowadays there are a bewildering number of trade weed killers and most effective they are. We use a paraquat diquat mixture for killing green rubbish and a CIPC residual spray for the control of germinating weed seed. As in all garden operations, we spray as little as possible; though our acres are insignificant in the countryside around us, we do feel that we should protect birds and wild life from the toxic effects of spraying. The minute amounts of the poison that can eventually kill or virtually sterilize a species of bird makes one realize how easily we could destroy many wild things for all time.

Provided one acts in time weeding nowadays in a small garden may be reduced to a few squirts of spray as one might with an aerosol spray inside the house. Mulching too does so much to combat weeds and increase the quality of the soil texture that it can hardly be emphasized enough.

Chapter 3

Guide Lines for Design

The title of this chapter is intentionally not too dogmatic. 'Principles of Design' sounds authoritarian and so frightening that one may think that there are absolutes of right and wrong in garden design. Now I do believe that there are certain things to be avoided and that certain methods are more likely to lead to a successful final result, but in gardening as in painting there are no set of arbitrary rules which will inevitably give the right result. The fact is that every garden poses different problems and every gardener will be striving for slightly different results. What would be right for one garden would be disastrous for another. If I err on the dogmatic side, take leave to disagree; I put the suggestions strongly because I believe them valid. There are some things to avoid. Never plant a Monkey Puzzle Tree below the study window.

The value of this chapter hinges on the definition of four words and their interpretation in the forming of the garden. Boldness, simplicity, balance, and foresight.

Even in a small garden the bold effect, the strong line, strong masses is what I think should be aimed at. Of course one cannot achieve the avenue of trees of the stately home and garden, we cannot harness Capability Brown's feeling for the ideal landscaped parkland. But there are simple things that can be

33

done to make the most of our precious square yards. Most gardens will allow a good proportion of their space to a lawn and even in such a basic thing as this there are points to remember. I believe that lawns should lead on into the garden, or that they are panels set into the design. The fresh green sward that we hope to maintain should be pleasing at all times and whilst this will depend to an extent on the mixture of seed used to sow the lawn and the trouble taken in its upkeep, it is mainly the shape of the lawn which is going to satisfy the eye or continually hit a jarring note. Except in the most formal circumstances a square shape is not satisfying. If a square lawn is decided on, it should be well framed by a broad path or deep borders and would be best if it gave way to beyond a further substantial area of grass.

In most gardens the lawn of oblong shape is best, the most usual vantage point of the lawn being at one end of the lawn. Presumably this point would be a window of the house. To exaggerate the length of the lawn, or rather its apparent length, it may well be worth touching up the natural perspective effect by making the far end of the lawn narrower than the near end. Even in a lawn of some thirty-feet length, the narrowing of the lawn by a foot or two will have quite a considerable effect in increasing the apparent length of the green sward. For reasons of upkeep and sometimes in a feeling for tidiness the usual choice of lawn shape is rectangular. But it is by no means always the most worthwhile shape to have. Once can gain the benefits of false perspective, giving distance and depth to the garden, just as well and perhaps more satisfyingly by having curving outlines to the lawn. This does not mean to cut a weaving wavy edge to the lawn but rather to make the outline on one side a simple curving line and on the other a gentle 's' shape. The result of this shape can be the chance to form a fine border feature at one side and to allow the eye to follow the tapered end of the lawn to a further prospect.

The type of seed mixture for the lawn depends entirely on the use to which it is to be put. With young children pitching Wigwams on it or using it as a sports field the grass is going to have to stand a considerable pounding, a cheaper hard-wearing mixture is obviously desirable. The finest mixture without rye grass to give the bowling-green effect is fine for anyone who views the lawn as the crowning glory of the garden and is willing to tend it lovingly. Often these very fine grass mixtures need to be looked after carefully, especially in the summer or on light soil when the rather more delicate and restricted rootrun of the fine grasses can be affected more quickly by drought conditions. There are a multitude of merchants offering lawn-seed mixtures, and an established seed merchant with a reputation to maintain will soon advise on a suitable mixture. As in the whole sphere of gardening the seed is the least expense, so that it pays to get the right seed, the best for your purpose. Economizing over seed quality is the most short-sighted of all supposed economies.

I do not propose to detail how to make a lawn, for this can be found in many books and in articles in the gardening press. Our concern is the form of the lawn. If the lawn is a formal rectangular one we should make sure that the lawn does not contain depressions in it that are going to hold water after a shower and present us with continual problems. If the lawn does not lie in a true plane, then a slight crown effect will be useful in helping surface drainage. With a lawn of informal shape we can allow ourselves a little more freedom in the levelling of the ground before seeding. A slight rise in the level of the lawn, especially at the far end where it is leading to some further feature may be

A LAWN NARROWED AT THE BOTTOM OF THE GARDEN, GIVES ADDED LENGTH

very pleasing; from the eye-level of the average onlooker viewing the lawn from a seated position by a house window a rise in the lawn level of a foot over several feet length can give a considerable proportion more green grass to behold. What must be avoided is the danger already mentioned of creating artificial pools on the lawn everytime the heavens open. Also any rolling effect should be seen to be a deliberate part of the design of the lawn and garden and not just a mistake, and the angles of the ground should be gentle so that they do not interfere with the blades of the grass-cutting machinery.

The lawn has to be cut. It is therefore not a complete labour-saving part of the garden. The edges of the lawn also have to be kept in some form of order if the best effect is to be enjoyed. There are good tools for edging lawns nowadays, both ordinary hand tools and mechanised ones. The edges can also be main-tained by the lawn running up to a well-made path which it cannot encroach on, or by being edged with long-lived artificial edges made out of metal or other materials. I have seen one lawn most successfully contained by offcuts of $\frac{1}{8}$-inch thick plastic sheeting.

What should be emphasized I believe is that a lawn to be effective should be a reasonable size, that normally the length should be at least a third longer than the width, and that only the largest lawn can be cut into without destroying its best effect. Beds cut into lawns are almost always a mistake. They destroy the peaceful unspoilt carpet effect of the lawn, and they create a lot more lawn edges to be kept in order or to get out of hand.

If the lawn is to be cut into at all, I suggest that it should be done simply and towards the end and perhaps one side of the lawn. There seems no point at all to me in cutting into the lawn merely to fill the space with bedding plants that may look bright for a few weeks in the year and to be left with a scar in the lawn for the rest of the time. Though I expect many, if not most, gardeners will take issue with me, I do not think even roses should be allowed to enter the lawn proper in a bed. Though the floribundas bloom for many weeks through the summer and are wonderful value, even these gay characters remain bare for months through the winter months and lack any real form or grace in their period out of active growth and bloom. The hybrid teas are of course even worse viewed from the 12-month angle. It may be argued that a rose bed cut into the lawn is permissible

LAWN EDGINGS

PLASTIC OR METAL STRIP

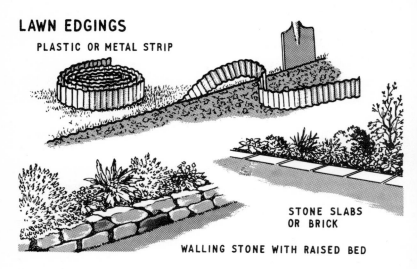

STONE SLABS OR BRICK

WALLING STONE WITH RAISED BED

if it contains other plants that will give interest and variety at other times, and of course this does lessen my objection to them. Many friends and customers of ours buy daffodils and grow these in rose beds so that there are at least two periods at which the plot of earth is giving forth plenty. It is a compromise, but it is not to my mind the real answer. I believe that if an incision is to be made in the green of the lawn it should only be done to afford a contrast that at all times will accentuate the character and beauty of the lawn.

The lawn is flat and a lively bright green. The contrast to this would be something vertical and a differing colour shade. We could plant a tree or a shrub. It may be that we could have enough room to plant a group of three shrubs or trees with the idea of eventually removing two of the three to allow the remaining one more room to expand and form the specimen that will just be the ornament that brings to life the splendid simple green dress of the lawn. Planting three, with the idea of sacrificing two, may seem extravagant but it will ensure that in the first few years some feature is made that does not look entirely niggardly. It may be that having three together may help one protect the other from the elements. It may be that in the end none are sacrificed, the three shrubs may join together and function as one. This is of course assuming as I do that three plants of the same species are planted. It may even be that these three can be planted close together and stay friends. Three Silver Birches close planted can look very well and one may get the branches twisting in competitive contortions that make them all the more interesting than even the most symmetrical and perfectly balanced tree.

If trees or shrubs are to be planted in a lawn for a contrasting specimen effect one must think to the future and make sure that the tree chosen is not some forest giant that is going to far outgrow its childhood home. One has got to think of the winter as well as the growing months. The bark and the pattern of bare branches of a deciduous tree should give pleasure through the winter, or one should plant an evergreen that will form a bold mass above the simple plane of the lawn. With shrubs the problem is the same, but perhaps being smaller, there is even more to be said for choosing an evergreen. We need not look for especially rare or unusual species. A group of three laurustinus, the *Viburnum tinus* so beloved by our grandparents, is still a most worthy plant. Though somewhat slow growing it will provide just that dark, rich green to contrast with the lawn that we need and of course it provides its plentiful crop of blossom in the winter months just when we most need something to enjoy. We might get the real exaggerated contrast of the vertical with the horizontal lawn by using an upright conifer, the column effect of the silver-grey green Irish Juniper, *J. communis hibernica*, if one is willing to wait for the rather slow rate of growth. *J. communis pyramidalis* forms a rather wider cone-like form.

The Irish Juniper may suggest a simple piece of sculpture and this prompts the thought that it may well be that we should use our lawn as a setting for a piece of sculpture. At the major flower shows there are firms that offer what are termed as garden sculptures. To me the vast majority of these are gross and offensive and cannot add much to the garden. My suggestion is that it may not be possible to get Henry Moore interested in a commission for your back garden or mine, but there are a multitude of young people of ability at the many art schools throughout the country who would be happy to undertake just such work. They hold shows of their work at least once a year and here you may spot just the thing that you want to create the focal point in the lawn. Normally the simpler abstract pieces are going to be the most effective.

If we decide we are not going to plant a piece of sculpture but want a living tree or shrub, we should cut out a piece of the lawn almost as wide as the branches of the tree or shrub and keep this circle of soil open for the years whilst the tree is establishing itself. Later this area of soil can be seeded with grass and the more complete effect of the lawn regained.

Boldness being effected in the lawn, we may now turn to the other features. First, although we have already discussed them in some length, we should perhaps emphasize the matter of paths. We do not want to give the effect of a motorway going up the garden, but on the other hand nothing is so continually irritating as a path that is too narrow to comfortably wheel a two-wheeled barrow along or to walk along in comfort with a friend. At the far end of the garden, where the lines of communication are of secondary importance it may be that a single line of 2-foot wide paving slabs will amply suffice, but normally the main paths of the garden need to be 4 feet across to provide easy and comfortable access. Where space is very limited a 3-foot width could suffice.

Where there is need of wider areas of permanent paving it is best to err on the bold larger size. The paved area near the house should be big enough to accommodate the garden chairs and tables that you hope you will have use for this coming summer. The simple paved area is made more impressive by containing it with a low wall, allowing of course an entrance to lawn and garden that is plenty wide enough. This low wall can often be one of the most enjoyable features of the garden, for it could be made a hollow wall or in reality a raised bed in which, whatever the weather, a wide variety of small plants can be grown and looked at. It is not the place for vigorous roses that are going to screen the rest of the garden during the summer, but it could be the home of a collection of alpine plants or alternatively a varied

PATH EXPANDED TO FORM SPACE FOR SEAT

lot of plants grown for their contrasting foliage. In shaded areas it may be the place to grow a collection of hardy ferns that will provide colour and form throughout the year.

The paths that go down the garden may well be expanded in width at certain strategic points to provide room for a garden seat that is so much more satisfactory placed on a solid base than on grass, or there may be an area close to a greenhouse, frames, summer house, or small kitchen garden where it helps to have extra room for barrows, baskets or merely for the look of the thing and to give room for admiring visitors to pause to see the rock garden, pool, marrows or other garden feature.

I am a believer in paths and paved areas. In this country of ours it so often rains, or threatens to rain, or has just rained, that it pays most handsome dividends to have solid ground under ones feet, for we do go into the garden even in bad weather even if it is merely to gather a few flowers, vegetables, or feed the birds. I am sure that it is cheaper to have a paved area than to have a lawn. A paved area costs about 1/6d. a square foot to lay down and it is there for all time, with no upkeep say the occasional sweeping of dead leaves and dust. A lawn requires considerable effort to make; it requires an outlay on seed and on a machine to maintain the grass at the regulation height. The machine will require looking after and servicing, the lawn will probably need applications of weed killer and fertilizer. But above all, the grass will need considerable hours of time over the year and years to keep it looking at its best.

This is not to say that I do not like grass lawns. I do. But I would suggest that anyone with a small garden might well consider whether it is worth the effort and the expense of time and money in making a lawn when a paved area might serve as well and be both more economic and more useful at all times of the year. Such a paved area is not necessarily a place without plants, creeping small plants like thymes may be allowed to carpet parts and one or more of the large tubs or similar containers now made

43

in a wide variety of materials may be planted up with shrubs, plants like geraniums or be used to contain miniature gardens of alpines.

One of the key words I suggested was boldness, another is simplicity. Perhaps the meaning of the two overlap as applied to garden design. We draw our plans in bold strong lines and shapes. It is often the simple effects that are created that are the most pleasing so that we might pause to think just what these simple effects are. We have already mentioned the single tree growing from the lawn. But we could expand this to suggest that the whole of the front garden might be lawn with just this one tree. What tree we might use depends on taste and some suggestions are listed and discussed in a later chapter on trees. We would not plant it centrally but to one side and perhaps towards the boundary away from the house. But of course the tree should not be planted so close to public or other private boundaries that the branches or the roots may form an obtrusive nuisance. It is of course not always the ideal perfectly-balanced tree that makes the best specimen tree in such a position. The Silver Birch whose main leader has broken close to the ground, and has three competing trunks stretching upwards, makes a far more interesting and satisfying picture. The flowering cherry is the obvious choice, if an almond has not already been chosen, and certainly few trees can compete with these in their flowering season. However there is sometimes a little stereotyped, rather ordinary look about these trees out of blossom, certainly in young trees that have yet to gain some character from their very age. My suggestion here is that it may well be best to try to obtain specimens of almond or cherry that have not been taken up with a single leader, to get a shrub shaped one and let it find its own shape, or even to take the saw or secateurs and encourage two or three branches to break low down. Alternatively one can look for a tree that always has some interest. I am very fond of the twisty Hancow Corkscrew Tree, the willow called *Salix matsudana tortuosa*. This like most willows grows rapidly but it forms a most graceful tree of curiously twisting stems that against the winter sky cut intricate and curious jigsaw patterns.

The smaller front garden is often difficult to manage in design terms partly due to its very smallness and also because of the dominance of the house. One way to clothe this plot simply is to devote it entirely to a collection of heathers. You may think this is rather a dull idea, but it is surprising what colour effects one can get with even only the foliate of heathers from their bright golds to every shade of green until almost black. Their shapes too do allow quite a bit of variation of the form of the miniature heathland. Some creep very close to the ground and do not rise above a very low carpet, but others whilst spreading do not ignore the vertical plane and come up six or nine inches whilst going several times the width. Other heathers form upright bushes. Of course the greatest variation can be gathered together where the soil is free from lime, but, even where there is lime, there are quite a number of *Erica carnea* varieties and all these are tolerant of lime as well as the hybrid *E. darlyensis*. The occasional small conifer between the heathers can add interest and looks completely in keeping.

The purist may feel that heathers are plants of the wide open moor tops and that as such they look best away from bricks and mortar. Personally I like heathers anywhere and they certainly look well by pathside or near the house. But there is perhaps a lesson to be learnt from such a garden full of heathers, and it is that there is some magic factor that produces a sum of beauty and satisfaction in a compound interest fashion. One heather looks well, two heathers look more than twice as well, four heathers look more than twice as well as two heathers and so on.

My business and my pleasure is growing daffodils. In no other flower is this rule of planting in numbers perhaps so fully apparent. A row of daffodils planted along a path or lawnside with a single bulb stationed at maybe fifteen-inch intervals is a pathetic sight. They are not policemen or soldiers placed to keep the border in order. How very much better to group the daffodils in one or two generous clumps. Here the gregarious flowers find their real beauty.

But this does not apply to one or two plants to the exclusion of others. This is one of the points that I would make a rule of design.

The rule of Three

Most gardeners have the collecting instinct. Their interest is aroused in a family of plants, and then it become easy to allow an almost obsessional desire to take hold to collect as many kinds of the family as possible. Even those with a more mild attack will usually have one plant each of three different varieties rather than three plants of one. There is always going to be this desire, but from the garden design point of view I feel that it is almost always best to pick out the one winning plant and buy three of this. Planted in threes you have more than three times the beauty of the single plant. You prevent the ever present possibility of bittiness in the border. With three of plants, shrubs and trees if possible, there is a cohesive effect to the design.

Obviously where smaller plants are being put into their places a group of more than three is best. Polyanthus and most primulas are best planted in dozens if not hundreds. The point is not to lose all sight of the beauty of a plant by having too little of a good thing. If it means that one has to get rid of some plants or resist the temptation to get others, then of course this is another of the inexorable lessons of gardening. All gardening is a form of selection. One selects plants from weeds, then the process is never ending. Alas, like morality, there are no sets of rules applicable in all circumstances and at all times, one is forced to choose.

The Winter

I believe that the case could be argued fairly, and almost con-clusively, that the best time to judge a garden's design is in the months of winter. For in Britain winter often begins in October and lasts well into March if not April. This gives us at least five months of the year as winter. The spring, summer and autumn will normally be a period of activity amongst our plants, and there will usually be plenty of interest to keep our hands active and our eyes filled. I contend that it is a poor garden that, with the frost that blackens the dahlias, is left destitute of interest until 'King Alfred' nods his head again. If we design the garden for the winter months it is sure that the other months will take care of themselves. Now having delivered myself of this dictum, what can we do to ensure interest through the winter.

Assuming for a start that we have paid thought to and con-

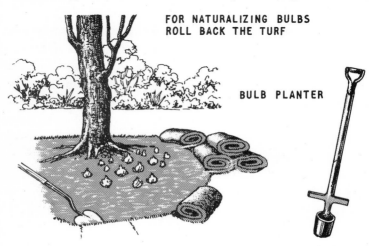

FOR NATURALIZING BULBS
ROLL BACK THE TURF

BULB PLANTER

structed features that will look well at any time such as walls, screens, steps, pergolas, and the statue of Lloyd George on horseback, I take it as axiomatic that we should look to shrubs and trees to provide us with our greatest interest outside during the winter. The lady of the house inside is busy bringing back the victoriana. Maybe we should look to what our Victorian ancestors were doing, or having done, outside in the garden.

48

Of course they had their Crystal Palace conservatories with hot house plants freshly gathered from the far flung parts of the empire and trading posts elsewhere. But they did not stop here. In the open garden beside the gravel paths were the shrubberies. Maybe these were a little heavy and funeral for our taste, perhaps the law of secateur and shears kept such toparian order as to repress character in shrub or tree to respectable rounded or squared conformity. But it is certain that the lord and master would see forms and colour in the garden as he left home for his counting house. Box, yew, holly, privet, aucuba, and conifers would be on parade, and not such a bad parade at that with all the variety to be found especially in families like the hollies and the vast numbers of conifers. Even the ivy was dragooned in its adult shrub-like form to salute evolution's greatest wonder.

Did they pick the flowers off their rhododendrons, too bright and frivolous in such a serious and earnestly progressive age. Probably not.

I think we should plant a few conifers. In the small garden we cannot achieve a forest. Maybe we could content ourselves with three of the cypressus's, now *Chamaecyparis,* probably picking a *lawsoniana* variety like *columnaris glauca* to spire upwards at the sky with rich blue-green foliage to make a background for other things less tall. We plant the conifers to the end of the garden for they may well be the tallest thing in it before we lay our spade to rest. We plant them in a triangle, not a straight line, if we have room we can allow all their full time but we know that two of the three may have to be axed on November 4th in ten years' time.

Somewhat to the other side, to form a balancing mass of green, we may plant a group of *rhododendrons*, the evergreen kinds. There are plenty to choose from, the old ones still holding their own for the great period of shrub hybridization was from the last century till the outbreak of the First World War. Since then breeders have turned their attention to annuals. 'Pink Pearl' will be there doubtless, maybe the red 'Britannia' and 'Purple Splendour.'

But again we should not forget the evergreen viburnums, *V. tinus* I have mentioned before. *V. 'Chenault'* might well be chosen with its dark green glossy leaves and wide rounded clusters of pink-tinted white flowers finely scented. The various evergreen berberis species and hybrids can take a place in the mixed border and help to give it shape when herbaceous plants have died down.

Once I despised the spotted-leaved *Aucubas* but now I can enjoy them and find the yellow and green foliage useful, healthy and attractive through the year. Not all the dislikes of youth last, then the aucubas seemed attacked by some malignant shrubby virus diseases and I did not like them. The Monkey Puzzle Tree is still a Monkey Puzzle Tree, a joke by the Creator, but not for my garden. Is it its fearful symmetry that has always jarred on me? I am not sure. The question of symmetry is one I must come back to.

Yet another childhood hate was the privets. Now, where I find in farm hedgerows the bunches of purple berries I cannot find it in my heart to condemn such a common plant, though I would not plant it as a hedge where it will not fruit. The golden privet is a most useful plant. Here again I would not think to plant a hedge of it, but a single bush, not clipped into a monstrous ball, but allowed some freedom to provide its bright golden-leaved branches throughout winter as well as any other month. What housewife with such a bush has not blessed it many times when short of foliage or flowers indoors. It is a bright and useful thing, and if it is common so let it be, it deserves to be for it brings brightness into the winter and it can easily be contained in the summer.

The conifers too do not restrict their pallette to pure greens, but have several golden variants that will also help lighten the winter day. Lawson's Cypress has several golden forms, 'Golden King' being a strong one and '*hillierii*' another graceful kind. There are a number of new golden conifers which will shortly be available and so it is worth asking the advice of a good shrub nurseryman before ordering.

As with other unusual colour variants, like copper leaved ones, I do not think it is wise to overplant the golden-leaved evergreens. One lightens up the garden, giving contrast and complementing the more natural greens, but if many golden leaved ones are planted the lighting effect becomes garish like neon lighting and everything suffers.

Evergreens give us our strong masses, and it is difficult to over emphasize their importance, but the deciduous trees and shrubs also give form in the winter garden. I am not very tidy minded, and never tie my daffodil leaves in knots, so that I enjoy a wild looking thicket. Some of the rose species that throw a fountain of viciously armed arching stems can make an unusual feature, certainly looking a whole lot more decorative than their hybrid cousins. The hardy bamboos with their strong upright growths and dark green leaves are pleasing. The appearance of health is half the pleasure. With *Viburnum fragrans* the strong upright growths continue to come each year intensifying the thicket but some arch outwards and so the rounded bushes broaden. A branch touches the ground and rotting starts a fresh fountain of strong brown stems. But as it provides scented posies of flowers in the winter it is doubly welcome, though, where formerly we would plant this, we now dig in bits of *V.x bodnantense* 'Dawn' which is more vigorous still and has larger bunches of winter flowers.

Again we get vigour and colour in winter from the coloured barks of willows that are cut back every other year to promote strong new growth. The Dogwoods also help, and some of the *Rubus* species with their white or yellowish-brown raspberry stems.

In planting our hedges too we will have the winter effect to think about. If we have time to wait a holly or a yew hedge will give us the dark background in front of which to plant some groups of white daffodils, or clumps of the paler hellebores. We might even think of using a form of Lawson's cypressus for a hedge for this is one of the conifers that will break out again when cut back. There is certainly something distinctive and enjoyable in the aromatic resinous smell of conifers as one brushes by. But few hedges to my mind can look so well as a neatly groomed beech hedge. It has many advantages. It grows quite quickly but is easily cut. It has not got the thorns and prickles of hawthorn or holly. It makes a good windbreak or screen in all months of the year. It responds well to the shears, and can be formed neatly so that the top is very nearly pointed and is certainly much narrower than at the base, and it is not difficult to keep the hedge well furnished to the ground. The plants are not expensive to buy and will grow well in almost all soils. But perhaps most important of all is the attractive foliage of the hedge, few young leaves have a more soft, bright and attractive green. The mature colour is pleasing, and most important of all the foliage when it turns its warm rusty-brown in the autumn remains there through the winter except in exceptional instances. The warm colour of the winter hedge can alone keep the garden looking bright in the winter. Through the summer months the bright green of the hedge can be further enhanced if, when originally planted, a few copper beech plants were added here and there. One copper to twelve ordinary beech would be plenty, and to my eye it would be best if the copper beeches were scattered apparently at random through the hedge so that perhaps there might be one copper then fifteen plain, another copper, followed by four plain, a copper, another eleven plain, a copper, etc. The dark foliage of the copper just adds the dark tone to highlight the bright fresh green of the standard.

Balance and symmetry

There have been times when the garden was treated like a carpet and made in perfectly symmetrical shapes and masses. I am never happy with any too detailed attempt at symmetry. An avenue of trees, or a grass path with hedges both sides, even perhaps with similar borders in front of the hedges, this is one thing and often a most happy and satisfactory piece of planting, but a wide stretch of garden properly laid out like a lifesize board for some crazy game this is something quite different. The avenue of trees or the hedged path, have a purpose, they lead somewhere. Where symmetry is carried out for the sake of some pathological sense of tidiness or a strangled creative sense then the thing is doomed. Only as an adjunct of some huge classical building where nature must be groomed in most formal attire to reflect the feeling of the building may this symmetry be excusable. But then this is not so much gardening as a hybrid between indoor decoration and architecture.

Symmetry is always in a threatened state. If a plant dies on the right side it must be replaced or the left-hand side one removed. When a tree becomes diseased, its fellow on the other side is in jeopardy. No; symmetry is too dangerous for me, and in any case what adventure is there for the eye that knows that what is on one side is mirrored exactly on the other.

But to say that I have no time for symmetry is not to say that I do not consider balance one of the principles of good design. Looking down the vista of the garden, perhaps down the lawn, we notice a group of three evergreen shrubs to one side and lower to the other side there is a thick clump of bamboo or a mass of some berberis. The one is balanced by the other but it is not a matter of being completely the same in weight and form and not at equal distances. The effect should be such that the

54

eye is taken from one mass to another, from one feature to another. The aim is for an interplay of shapes, habits, colours, sizes, and characters that contrast with each other and create an interaction. There is balance, but not the perfect balance of symmetry, rather that balance that leaves a degree of tension in the play.

Contrast and surprise

We have already several times alluded to the possibility of the use of contrast in our design. Often the most attractive use of contrast is in the grouping of plants of differing shape and with markedly different foliage in shape or colour. In colour we may have that useful all round the year shrub, *Senecio laxifolius*, with its wide ranging masses of silver-grey leaves in a sunny spot in front of a dark wall of yew. This *Senecio* is a real stalwart shrub, perhaps a rather sprawly character, but this can be corrected by continually pinching out the top growths and making the shrub more compact and bushy.

On a small scale the various *Sempervivums*, *Sedums* and *Saxifragas* can make a wonderfully varied living mosaic of colour and form. Some of the *Tulipa greigii x T. kaufmanniana* hybrids might well be grown for their grey foliage striped with purple to contrast with the low masses of bright green mossy saxifrages. *Hostas* in bright and dark green, wide-leaved and arching over close to the ground, will provide the contrast of colour and shape for the upright swords of iris be they the narrow rapiers of some of the species like *I. chrysographes* or the broad-swords of Bearded Irises.

55

The idea of using contrasts of form and colour creates too the element of surprise. But possibly in garden planting we get our surprises from the plant that we come on unexpectedly, a group of gentians providing a pool of deep blue just behind a berberis species, a flight of blue poppies holding their blooms to earth by 3- or 4-foot stems between two flanking shrubs, even a group of three or more giant sunflowers towering over the gardener.

ge plants in a small town garden

An example of statuary in a town garden

Chapter 4

Some Garden Features

Excluding life-sized statues of Lloyd George on horseback or 20-foot replicas of the Eiffel Tower made out of matchsticks, we are still left with many important garden features. It may well be that the walls of the garden or the paths are themselves major features in the design. Certainly we hope that the plants themselves are important factors. Though, it is mentioned elsewhere, the plots that are usually called borders should be so formed as to be a sensibly proportioned feature. The word border suggests edging or, boundary and certainly a narrow strip devoted to a thin line of herbaceous plants is hardly going to prove a feature. Better by far to scrap one border entirely and double the width of the other. Alternatively in a small garden where the windows look directly over the plot, the major border could be across the plot with the sides devoted to wall plants, so maybe giving the effect of looking out at a stage set. But this chapter is devoted to dealing briefly with some of the possible manufactured features of the garden.

Raised beds and hollow walls
The usefulness of these in bringing the level of the garden somewhat closer to that of homo sapiens might be charted in the falling incidence of lumbago and slipped discs, or it may be

measured in the increased pleasure to be gained by examining and working with some wide range of plants that can be grown at this height in the world. Certainly such beds may be insurance against failing interest in the garden as age creeps up on one. Again I make the point that a garden on several levels is much richer in design possibilities than one laid out like a table-cloth.

By the paved area near the house it is likely that we could usefully divide this from the garden proper by a hollow wall. It will

RAISED BEDS BREAK UP THE FLATNESS

give us a chance also of constructing a pleasant stepped entrance-way into the garden. I am assuming that a hollow wall may have a foot or 15 inches of soil width before it starts to become a raised bed. The reason for making the distinction is that where the two sides containing the soil are close we shall be able to have a common solid bottom of concrete and we can also tie both sides together as we build up the walls.

58

SOME GARDEN FEATURES

The material we use for the walls will vary from ordinary domestic bricks to pieces of rock and will include some of the prefabricated slabs made especially for this purpose. What is used will depend on the effect to be produced and the surroundings. Normally the site of the wall would be pegged out and the soil removed for 4 or 5 inches depth and about 4 inches extra width each side. The concrete is then worked into this foundation using a mix of approximately one cement to three sand and five aggregate by volume. When the foundation has hardened the walls may be built up a course at a time, checking carefully to make sure that one is following the line wanted, be it straight or curved. The line of the wall can be scribed easily on the foundation. If the wall is not to be absolutely vertical then obviously the lean in from one side should the the same the other side. At ground level there will have to be left drainage holes every 2 or 3 feet. Having given the mortar of the walls time to harden the centre may be filled and the top planted. It is best to have plenty of drainage even in this narrow strip of garden, a good proportion of peat can be worked into the top soil to help retain the moisture. Just how careful one is with the compost may depend a little on the plants that are to be featured here. A row of geraniums will not need a very rich soil mix, alpines will want perfect drainage, bulbs and bedding plants will take almost any soil.

Where rock is used for the wall, it will be possible to allow a slight lean backwards on both sides and to leave occasional cavities to be planted later. This is of course not the same as a retaining wall built of rock which holds back a higher level of

59

soil in the garden and may be treated in a somewhat different way.

Raised beds will be made of a size to fit in with the garden design, but for ease of working one not much more than 5 feet across will allow one to reach all parts without much trouble. The height will depend on the position of the bed in the garden,

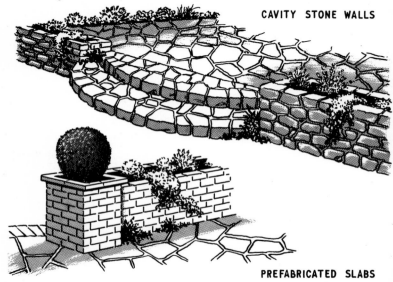

CAVITY STONE WALLS

PREFABRICATED SLABS

and the purposes for which it is being built, and on the disposition of the builder. The closer it is to 2 feet high, the easier it will be for the less active gardener to look after. A rise of at least a foot is really necessary to give oneself a chance of making the most of the bed and for it to play an obvious part in the garden plan.

60

One of the most satisfying of uses for these raised beds is to devote them to rock garden plants. A rock garden requires quite a lot of building, a considerable amount of maintenance, and can be quite expensive if any quantity of good rock is used. A rock bed in which a more or less flat level is given some contouring and interest with small rocks is quite easy to maintain and it is perhaps an even easier medium in which to manage a collection of very interesting and attractive dwarf plants. The essential

BUILDING A ROCKERY

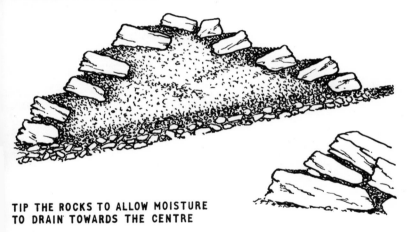

TIP THE ROCKS TO ALLOW MOISTURE TO DRAIN TOWARDS THE CENTRE

factor in the building of such a bed is to make sure that the drainage is perfect. These alpines are often intolerant of poor drainage around their necks as well as at their toes, so, having provided sharp drainage below, the soil mixture used above should be very quick draining also. A substantial quantity of grit in the soil mix will help to get the water away from the leaves of a plant that may in nature grow only on the scree sides of mountains where they live on virtually nothing. They do have fantastically long root systems and can find the moisture they need from feet or even yards below.

A rock bed may be built up with walls of rock and of course

ROCKS ARRANGED IN A NATURAL DESIGN . NO STRAIGHT EDGES

this is ideal. The walls will be built with the larger pieces forming the bottom course, the next layer being a little further back and each rock covering the join in two below. I would advocate bedding some of the rocks with cement concealed as much as possible. This avoids any possibility of the walls breaking away. Naturally it is pleasant to see plants growing out between rocks so that many of the spaces between the rocks may be planted as one builds up the wall.

But a rock bed can be planted in a bed built up with ordinary bricks without looking incongruous. A brick wall some 18 inches above ground may be partially draped by trailing plants coming over the side, without leaving spaces for planting up the sides.

PLANTS FOR THE ROCKERY

AUBRETIA

PRIMULA DENTICULATA

ARMERIA THRIFT

One must remember to leave drainage spaces in such walls at the bottom.

A dry wall, built of rock layers leaning back and containing the soil of a higher level of the garden, will provide another chance to grow some of the stronger growing rock garden plants. Such simple easy plants as *Semperviviums* and *sedums* can look most attractive in a mixed collection. Hardy ferns will do well where there is a fairly constant supply of moisture and where such a banked rise does not face the very hottest un-shaded sun. Pinks with grey foliage look pleasing out of bloom.

These little plants can be grown without the space one would need for a rock garden or bed by selecting a few to group in a miniature garden. These can be created out of old domestic sinks if one is not going to go to the expense of buying one made of rock. The glaze can be covered and the appearance of

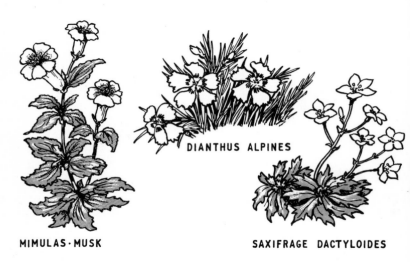

DIANTHUS ALPINES

MIMULAS·MUSK   SAXIFRAGE DACTYLOIDES

natural stone created. Having cleaned one of the old glazed sinks of all dirt and especially of all grease, the outside surface, the rim and the first few inches inside are covered with one of the modern bonding agents, such as Uni-bond or Polybond. When it has just started to dry, but is still tacky, a mixture of what is called Hypatufa is applied to the surface. This hypatufa is

RUSTIC ARCH

LONICERA · HONEYSUCKLE

WISTARIA SINENSIS

STONE PERGOLA

made out of these materials by bulk, one cement, one sharp sand, and two sifted sphagnum peat. It is mixed with just enough water to make it easy to apply to the sink without it running off. The final effect is a very approximation to one of the old stone troughs hewn out of solid rock, indeed they can easily be taken for the original stone product.

Pergolas and pillars

A complete pergola with the covered paved pathway may be a possibility, but a more likely design would be a single line of columns running alongside a path or built behind a border. This gives one the chance of growing many of the climbing plants that can give a new dimension to the garden. A single row of pillars linked at the top with a row of rafters might be used as a screen with the strong growing Virginia Creeper, Parthenocissus vitacea, going along the rafters and sending down long hanging stems as a curtain. Roses can add to the colour, as can plants of Wisteria.

Even where a row of pillars with rafters may be out of the question, it may be that a circle of such pillars, or a semicircle, may provide height and interest in the garden.

Obviously the pillars must be well built; if of bricks or manufactured slabs the foundations must be firm and a few courses built up at a time. It may be more suitable sometimes to have a brick-built foundation coming up some 18 inches or so and this to house an upright pillar of wood well treated in preservative. Rafters along the top link the whole together, and this framework alone looks attractive and provides both the scaffolding for climbing plants and a picture frame for a shrub or piece of sculpture.

Pools

The use of prefabricated pools and liners of plastic sheeting has given everyone the chance of incorporating a pool in the garden design without the considerable labour and expense of building a concrete pool of either formal or informal design. Not that a pool just happens, the site has to be excavated. This pile of soil may be just what we want to build up the soil level elsewhere.

The site for the pool will probably be easy enough to decide, an informally-shaped one would certainly look better to one side of the garden. It may well be two-thirds the way down the garden with a path leading beside it. It may be a formal path or one made of stepping stones through the lawn. If this is decided on, the stones should be not less than 18 inches square and should be securely bedded in the ground so that the lawn-mower blade cutting the grass clears the top of the stones. Normally the pond will be clear of trees that will only be too ready to shed their leaves into the water. It is likely that we shall get the most pleasure from our pool if from the usual viewing side we have the margin more or less clear so that we see the water. Conversely it may well be that we can give more dramatic impact to the pool if at the far side we have a miniature cliff face of rock apparently rising out of the water and maybe reflected in it. Alternatively a semi-dwarf conical conifer or a group of three will give the same feeling.

Most pools will be of two levels, a shallow shelf being incor-

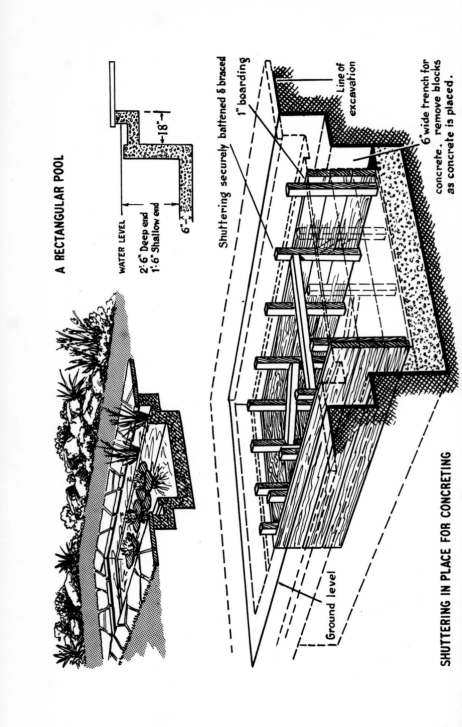

A RECTANGULAR POOL

WATER LEVEL

2'6" Deep end
1'6" Shallow end

18"

6"

Shuttering securely battened & braced

1" boarding

Line of excavation

6" wide trench for concrete, remove blocks as concrete is placed.

Ground level

SHUTTERING IN PLACE FOR CONCRETING

porated into the design to allow one to grow some of the attractive water plants that grow in the shallows. In the deeper water there will be the opportunity of growing one of the lesser vigorous water lilies. Whilst the pool needs plants growing in and around it for the most pleasing effect, it is very easy to overplant it and soon find that there is more leaf than water. We need most of the water clear, a mirror to sky and to the plants around. Around the margin of the pool we can plant some of the moisture-loving plants, for even though we do not have water perculating from a plastic pond to the soil around, it is probable that with the rainfall we have in this country some extra moisture will spill over the borders of the pool. Certainly it will look the right place to grow some of the moisture-loving asiatic primulas and irises even if one has an occasion to give them an extra ration of water.

We do need to empty the pool sometimes so that we must have arranged a drainage pipe from the bottom of the pool with a plug to release the water. We may be able to arrange to siphon the water away to some lower level.

It may well be that in the restricted space of the small garden that an oblong formal pool may be more in character, perhaps flanking one of the paved areas. Here the water may well be even more the main feature, its surface perhaps only broken by a solitary water lily and maybe an iris with its swordlike foliage to one side.

Water may dominate the whole garden, with paving around and stepping stones through it, or again it may make its presence felt only as a guggling small outlet of water falling over cobbles or rocks in an informal way or in severely sculptured pieces of formality. Such water can run its continuous course with the aid of a very small pump that is itself not dear and is inexpensive to run.

In the list of books given in the appendix, there are mentioned one or two that are devoted to garden pools.

Most of the manufactured pieces specially made as garden sculpture seem particularly poor in design. But certainly a simple sundial, or even a well-made garden seat can act as a garden feature. It would be interesting to see more modern sculptures in our gardens for their often simple forms might well exercise just that correct amount of dominance over their surroundings to stimulate without overwhelming.

Chapter 5

Planning for the Year

I have dignified this short section to chapter status, to emphasize a simple point that can get easily overlooked. It is never to early to start thinking about the garden design from the timepoints of our year. Nothing is so easy to do, almost unconsciously, as to produce a garden which is a glorious picture for a few weeks in summer. Many things conspire to make this so. First the variety of plants that bloom through the summer is greatest. The rose alone must take the blame for perhaps overemphasizing the central act in our garden play. We see more flowers in other gardens, we see more flowers at shows in the summer months, we visit the nurseries and garden centres in the spring and summer months, and so we naturally fall for the flowers and plants that are most effective when we see them.

It may be that the summer is the season when we expect to be out and to be enjoying the garden. We are not worried about other times. We expect to be viewing television, or busy with a hundred and one other social activities during the autumn, winter and early spring months. We do not expect to be out in the garden at these times. And if this is the conscious choice of the individual garden owner, who am I to argue against this. But I would point out that it rains in summer, that winter and autumn days can be as pleasing outside as many a summer or spring one. And I would argue that it is well to have some things in the garden that look well in the winter and do not leave it like a desolate unfurnished room for months on end.

I have said before that I believe that garden design should begin with the envisaged picture of the plot in winter. If we can have some form, some interest, some colour in the winter garden then the other seasons will look after themselves. Nothing very elaborate need be required. A few conifers and evergreen bushes will provide living furniture to the garden room. Perhaps in winter we may realize afresh that green is the basic colour of our palettes and that this is such a varied one that it can produce alone a refreshing and delightful picture. It is against a background of greens from the pale greys, through the range of polished or mat shades, to dark black-green of yew or holly that we expect any colour to add the focal points of floral interest.

Conifers like *C. glauca Spek* will sparkle with vivid silver-grey through winter and summer months. *C. lawsoniana alumii* in somewhat more greeny-blue shades add a darker shade, but the conifers are legion in shades of green and range in size from pygmy efforts for the sink garden to giant forest trees all in every shade of green from grey to nearly black and from apple-green to gold. Their forms too vary from the upright dark columns of the Irish Yew to the perfect cones of the apple-green *Picea albertiana conica* so slow growing, to such prostrate sweeping carpets as are formed by a number of Junipers like *J. horizontalis* or *J. sabina tamariscifolia*.

But greenery alone is not the only thing we see with clearer

72

he use of walls, flagstone patio and foliage plants

Hosta Sieboldii, Clematis Jackmanii, Golden Privet and *Miscanthus Saccharifolius*

beautiful setting for a small pool

Foliage border in a London garden

eye in winter, we note the forms of shrub and tree that much more precisely. Even such a common but worthy plant as *Cotoneaster horizontalis* we can enjoy with its herring bone pattern of branches. We may well have planted this against a wall as is so often done and with very good effect, but we could also have planted it nearby the patio or some paved area where the plant lives up to its name and builds up its intricate designs low over the soil surfaces and attractive sweeps across the edges of our paving. Such a plan might also have been effected with one of the low growing junipers. Higher we may see the curly branches of Harry Lauder's Walking Stick, the twisty hazel, *Corylus avellana contorta* or the similarly designed but taller twisty willow, *Salix madsudana tortuosas*.

We need not dwell on shrubs and trees as different plants are suggested for garden effect around the year. Shrubs and trees have their chapters and their contributions to the different seasons stressed.

Spring is of course only Nature's excuse for daffodils, and these bright flowers, so easy to grow and keep blooming year by year, are the leading characters in this act. They will be well backed by many flowering shrubs. Forsythias burst extravagantly into golden display, the almonds and cherries bring pink and white blossom, and rhododendrons in almost every shade add their aristocratic splendour to the show. Apparently nowadays it is common practice to buy in the heavily-budded large-flowered rhododendrons and plant them up even in soils where they cannot hope to reach maturity with lethal amounts of lime in the soil. They are treated as bedding plants, one season's flower or two and the owners are happy. It grieves me to think of this but maybe I am too old-fashioned to change my outlook. It may be that tomorrow's gardeners are going to change the garden decor as one might spring clean the house, a room here being repainted and new wallpaper hung, whilst outside the garden is remodelled for the current year. The plants are expendable bits of decor.

Daffodils are so numerous nowadays that it can be quite a task selecting the ones to grow. I have chosen a few that for garden purposes I feel are really worthwhile. I would expect them to bloom freely, to grow strongly, and provide variety in colour and form over many weeks of the spring. They will be planted with 3 or 4 inches of soil above their noses and with at least 4 inches between their bulbs and then left down for three or four years by which time they will have increased and have got so crowded as to need lifting, splitting and replanting again. 'Galway' is chosen as a traditional golden-yellow daffodil. Though classified as a large cup it is to all intents and for all garden purposes a fine trumpet daffodil with broad petals and noble trumpet. It is a rich deep yellow and the large flowers are freely produced, and are of fine smooth form, and last a long time. The foliage is dark and neat. It blooms early midseason.

'Armada.' This is a bright early flower, just the thing to open the brighter days of spring. It is a large flower and a strong free-blooming plant. It has wide golden petals and a large crown of rich tangerine orange.

'Kilmorack,' 'Ceylon,' or 'Straight Flush' might be chosen to take the orange and gold theme a little further into the spring for, although these open quite early, they are very good lasting plants and each has thick flat deep gold petals and neat goblet crowns of orange that becomes darker after opening. They are all neat strong plants.

TYPES OF NARCISSI

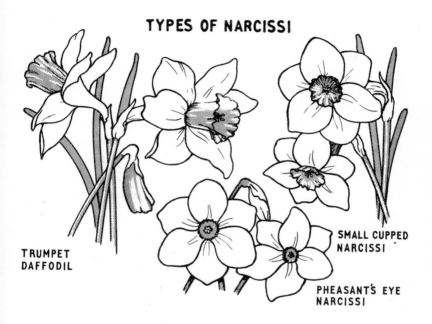

TRUMPET
DAFFODIL

SMALL CUPPED
NARCISSI

PHEASANT'S EYE
NARCISSI

For bicolour effect there are two plants that might be chosen. As an early kind 'Brunswick' with white petals and crowns of lemon is attractive and long lasting. Slightly later the white and deep gold of the trumpet kind 'Ballygarvey.' This gives crowds of well-formed large flowers, the wide white petals being triangular and held away at right angles to the trumpet with its rolled back brim.

Of very many white and orange flowers, one of the finest is 'Kilworth' which is a rather late flower, a large one with white petals perhaps just slightly milky white rather than frosty white. But the crown makes the flower, for it is a good size and a most rich brilliant shade of orange red. White and orange might also be represented by 'Geranium,' a many-headed tazetta type with rounded white flowers centred with small cups of bright orange. This is a late flower, and one that does well inside as well as in the garden.

The later daffodils are usually white petalled, 'Ballintoy' is not though it comes quite late and is a very smooth fine flower and grand plant. It is useful in having bright gold and orange flowers when most of these have finished. But the very latest of daffodils are whites. I would always have a group of the old fashioned 'Pheasant Eye Narcissus,' *N. poeticus recurvus*, however small the garden was. With its gracefully recurving petals and its neat yellow eyes edged red, it is a real delight, but of course it spoils us by providing us with one of the most pleasing of flower perfumes. Flowering at the same late season comes 'Frigid,' a most lovely jewel in pure snow white. It grows and blooms freely with wide triangular petals and small eyes all vivid white save for the rich green which lies in the centre of the cup.

I am not a fanatic about double daffodils. Some I positively dislike as shapeless abominations, but some of the newer ones are flowers of good character, not so overcrowded with petals as to be without form, not so heavy as to be blown to the ground by wind or the weight of rain. 'White Lion' is one of the finest of these garden-worthy doubles. It will stand the weather and has neatly formed flowers of white centred with intermingled petals of buffy primrose.

At one time there seemed to be a prejudice against white daffodils. This is certainly not so widespread nowadays. We

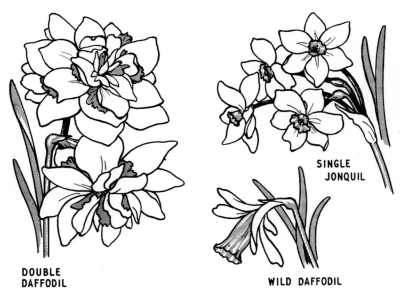

SINGLE JONQUIL

DOUBLE DAFFODIL

WILD DAFFODIL

find that we sell large quantities of whites. Always popular is 'Mount Hood' a vigorous white trumpet kind that is a nicely formed flower with good white petals and a well formed trumpet that opens cream and becomes white, this transformation is quicker and more effective some years than others. A flower

77

like 'Arctic Doric' opens absolutely white and remains white through its life. This is an early flower which grows easily and increases with great abandon in the same generous way in which it blooms. The petals are laid flat and shine white but the chaste crowns seem to be even more vividly pure, looking blue tinted in some lights.

Prejudices in flowers are always going to be present. Although it was before the First World War that breeders saw their first pink-tinted daffodils blooming, the general public often still expresses itself shocked by the 'unnatural' colour. I like all colours in daffodils. In the pinks I have several favourites. Of the lower priced kinds I enjoy 'Maiden's Blush' with its neat white perianth of flat petals and its trumpet-shaped crown quite richly painted pink. However undoubtedly the pink that is going to come more and more to the fore as the years go by is 'Passionale' which is an incredibly strong growing kind and one incapable of producing a poor flower. It has silken petals stretched flat in impeccable show form and a large beautifully balanced crown of rich pure pink untouched by hint of orange or lavender.

One of the newer departures in daffodil breeding have been the lovely lemon shaded flowers that excite such interest at shows and in gardens. Now quite well established is 'Binkie' a flower that opens lemon throughout with the crown a slight shade deeper, but which, as the days pass, undergoes a change so that before it dies the flower is lemon in the petal and white in the crown, the complete reverse of the usual pattern in daffodil colouring. Now, newer flowers of this colouring have been bred. 'Daydream' is an exciting new one with very rich lemon petals held perfectly flat and broad away from the large trumpet crown that becomes almost pure white and in shorter time than 'Binkie.' 'Charter' is an outstanding daffodil, it opens before any of the other reversed bicolours but is there on parade when these later flowers have been opened for a long time. It too opens all over lemon, but its crown soon loses its lemon colouring and shines white. The flowers are well posed, making the most of their unusual colouring over their long life. It is a magnificent daffodil.

Before leaving the daffodil family we should mention two kinds that might well grace every garden without becoming too common or the less welcome. Both are very early flowering kinds. 'The Tenby Daffodil,' *N. obvallaris,* is a small fellow, just 9 inches high but its flowers are relatively large. They are a uniform bright gold in neat flat perianth of petals and in bold trumpet nicely expanded and serrated. No daffodil is more trouble free. Once planted it will come up for ever and give more flowers each year with no further lifting. It lasts for a long time in the earliest weeks of spring. At the same time another character opens. This is 'Peeping Tom,' a taller flower, a foot to 15 inches high and with the most distinctive appearance. Very long narrow trumpets are relieved of the possibility of the accusation of snoutiness by the neat flange and serration at the brim, but the narrow character of the trumpet is further emphasized by the fly-away swept-back wing petals that give the flower its characteristic wind-swept but attractive appearance. The flowers might have been made of plastic so long do they last. It must be the longest lived daffodil in flower.

Tulips follow daffodils as the next dominant family in spring and though I like most tulips I would not worry about planting any nowadays except the species, the *kaufmanniana* hybrids or the magnificent race of flowers derived from the traditional Darwins crossed with *T. fosteriana*. These huge flowers are marketed as Darwin Hybrids. This is I believe a very bad name in that it suggests that the Darwin part of the parentage is the dominant factor when in reality the influence of the fine giant *T. fosteriana* is the thing that matters. Apart from the matter of appearance, what separates these new hybrids from other kinds is that one can plant these and expect them to come up two years or more without being lifted. Older types of tulips would have to be lifted to survive.

There are now, very many of the new Darwin Hybrid Tulips to choose from. 'Apeldoorn' is perhaps the one most often seen for it features in the florist's window as well as in the garden. It stands over 2 feet tall with huge orange scarlet flowers. These are flowers to look inside, in 'Apeldoorn' the large black base is ribboned with yellow. Now we have 'Golden Apeldoorn' a deep golden sport made all the more effective for this dark centre. 'Gudoshnik' varies the colour pattern, for though most of these new hybrids are in various dazzling shades of red, this is a deep yellow flower which is dotted and splashed with red to give a most pleasing effect. This again has sported and given what to my taste is one of the finest of the family, 'Jewel of Spring,' a huge sulphur-yellow flower with a dark olive or blackish-green base. The edges of the petals are just touched by a pencilled rim of red. 'Spring Song' has the virtue of opening rather before some and is a very sturdy large tulip of glowing vermilion warmed with a hint of crimson. 'Red Matador' is a vigorous tulip that increases in the garden. It is a shiny flaming deep scarlet red with a yellow base suffused with black pencilling. It too is early and will grow well under glass as well as in the garden.

The race of Water Lily tulips, the *T. kaufmanniana* hybrids, is a population explosion that provides us with such a wide choice that it is almost overwhelming. One wonders whether in fact too many seedlings have been named and whether it might not have been wiser to have distinguished by names a lesser number and so not confused the ordinary gardening public. However they are all so good it is difficult to carry through such a policy. Like an ordinary *T. kaufmanniana* writ large is 'Magnificent.' This has large flowers of white but with the outside of the petals painted rosy red to give long upward pointing buds set like candles and reaching some 8 inches high. More brilliant in colouring is 'Josef Kafka' an early deep gold flower made still brighter by having the outside petals coloured red and the centre too rimmed bright red. It is attractive too for the foliage which is low, broad, and much ornamented by the purple coloured striping along their length. 'Shakespeare' is one that I enjoy. It is quite a dwarf, and not one of the largest but its colouring is very pleasant, being a blend of pinky apricot, salmon and orange. 'Scarlet Elegance' is a rather small kind but an extremely floriferous one with bright red flowers. It comes early, stands 4 or 5 inches high and increases very satisfyingly over the years.

After the tulips come the pyrethrums, the lilies, the roses, irises and paeonies, all the flowers of the summer. June is the month of the paeony for me. These wonderful flowers in their many varieties seem to have all the qualities one might ask of a good herbaceous plant. It is a strong plant, virtually indestructible, a National Debt of a plant that gets bigger and bigger as the years go by and is there forever. In youth many varieties come through the ground with stems and young leaves glistening in glorious crimson shades, the mature leaves are boldly well designed, the aging leaves in autumn often paint themselves in colours to rival the brilliance of maples. The flowers have a sense of timing and occasion, the buds that rise with the leaves, tight small knobs that slowly, slowly gain in size, keep one in suspense awaiting their opening. Then suddenly, almost overnight, the great buds burst open and unfurl their silks. They make a study of white, for there are whites and whites, some icy, some cream, some white but emblazoned with crimson blotches. But if they make a study of white, of the permutations of pink shades they make a profession or an art, every pink is there from the most delicate of blushes to the richest of pinks that borders on the very threshold of red. But not only is every shade represented but a flower will open one shade and by slow, scarcely perceptible degrees change to other shades, running perhaps through a scale of colours till rich pink becomes white, but at no time does the flower not own a great beauty. This changing character of some kinds varies from season to season, the sun obviously plays its part, so that the changing colour may also depend on the amount of shade the flower has. Some kinds are far more steadfast in their colour. There are also the reds, the rich shades that range from the almost pink to the almost black-crimson of some. The form of the flower can vary from a single saucer shape with central boss of stamens through every degree of doubling up to the massive doubled balls that might have been a plaything for a small infant, a soft velvety round flower. With each flower is usually added its portion of scent for most of these flowers do have scent and many have a most rich gorgeous perfume that seems to evoke thoughts of more spacious days or make one dream of some Arcady where no pain and little effort have to be paid for measureless pleasure through long sunny perpetual summer days, a world with the experience and discernment of age and the vigour and freshness of youth.

Of the hundreds of paeonies, a garden, even a small plot of some yards, should have at least one. It might well be argued that even this solitary specimen should be a single paeony and, if so, then one of the strongest candidates for this selection would be 'Bowl of Beauty.' This is one of the so-called imperial paeonies, the single wide bowl of broad shining petals surrounds a central cluster of upright creamy-white petaloids, this central ornament contrasting and making all the more of the rich pink of the wide bowl.

'Sarah Bernhardt' is probably the best known of the double paeonies if one excuses the old double crimson that is not very satisfactory with its flowers fading in colour and having less grace than most of the main family of herbaceous paeony hybrids. 'Sarah Bernhardt' is of course a terrifically robust plant and will produce very good crops of large showy flowers of apple blossom pink each of the many petals tipped silver. It is an old trusted variety. A newer kind is 'Mrs. Roosevelt', a vigorous plant with finely produced flowers of luminous light pink formed of wide neatly arranged petals. Of the whites one could choose the magnificent 'Kelways Glorious' with its huge gleaming white flowers of most perfect doubled form and measuring six or seven inches across. Being both reliable and a free bloomer and possessor of a fine scent it lacks nothing. We are growing as well the newer kind Mrs. J. V. Edlund which is a most pleasantly formed flower, scented and both lovely in the garden and cut when it will last for ages. There are no buttercup yellow paeonies but a number are pale yellow. 'Duchesse de Nemours' is a sulphur or light yellow kind that is both prolific in bloom, fine in foliage, sweetly scented, and reliable. It fades to white like most of this colour, the stronger the sun the quicker they fade so that this is one for the shady spot. Fortunately paeonies are not fussy about their quarters. There are a number of flowers in the deep red end of the colour scale that are very worthy of a place in the garden, but I am very impressed by a relative newcomer a flower called 'Kansas' that has deep red blooms that are well formed and hold their colour very much better than most. Its petals have a high gloss sheen making them all vividly alive and, as they are produced with happy generosity, the plants are most effective.

Summer is the time for roses and for roses we have allowed a chapter. Let us pass to lilies. These in the middle of the hybridizing revolution are now becoming more and more

84

popular, though even now we have not arrived at the end of the line product, lilies that bloom in graceful beauty in clear colours with an abandon that they repeat without fail each year without care in any soil. But some kinds come near to this ideal. Early in the summer the Mid Century Asiatic hybrids brighten June, and July days with their bright colours. Still outstanding is the vivid range 'Enchantment' with its clusters of upward looking bright blooms. As good is 'Harmony' with slightly fewer flowers, more wide petalled, and a rich golden orange colour. Later come some of the rather more dainty types like the 'Citronella' strain with their five, six, or seven feet stems holding a lose pyramid of hanging deep lemon flowers with petals curled back and variously spotted with small dark touches.

The trumpet lilies are midsummer plants flowering from the end of June through July and August into September. The vastly popular *L. regale* is so vigorous that it is little wonder that it still holds its own in competition with the newer hybrids. Good strains of *L. regale* with wide petals are no mean beauties. However the new hybrids are exciting. 'Royal Gold' is a derivative of *L. regale* but in this strain the flowers are not white but rich shades of yellow. Taller and perhaps the finest trumpet shaped lily for general garden use is 'Golden Splendour,' for this is a really strong plant which may have five very large flowers on a stem but can have three or four times as many once it really gets going. As the flowers are huge and finely displayed on tall strong stems it cannot help making itself the centre of interest in the garden when it is in flower. Rather lighter and perhaps more refined in form is 'Limelight' in a cool lemon gold that is painted evenly over the long gently expanded and recurved trumpet petals. It is rather more gracefully posed in its stems than the strong 'Golden Splendour.'

Of the white lilies a tall huge flowered one is 'Black Dragon.' Inside it is dazzling white, outside the petals are a rich purple ribboned with white. Stems some six feet high can carry any number of flowers up to or over a full dozen. As each is probably more than six inches across a few spikes certainly make a show. The 'Black Magic Strain' is derived from 'Black Dragon' and as a strain the individual plants must of course vary they are all close to their mother in character.

'Pink Perfection' is the name given to a strain of trumpet lilies in which the pink, sometimes seen in small quantities on the back of such flowers as *L. regale,* has flooded over the whole flower and produced a most pleasing effect. They are all pleasant. 'Damson' is a clone in which this pink colouring is very deep, though the flower opens almost white inside it very soon assumes the dark fushia pink that makes this a very noticeable kind. The petals are tipped white and have a silver white sheen overlaying the pink, a most delicate and attractive glistening effect. The flowers may be up to seven inches across with each petal being five inches long and almost half as wide. The buds are deep plum coloured promises.

Many lilies continue to bloom into the autumn, the *L. speciosum* kinds bloom in August and September but for me the autumn is the time of Dahlias, Chrysanthemums, berries and foliage. We grow only a very few Dahlias and Chrysanthemums.

A few Dahlias provide huge lots of flowers for the border and for cutting. Not being a Chrysanthemum fanatic I cannot afford the time they need to grow a show bloom so that we only have a few spray types. But autumn berries and foliage is the autumn colour I enjoy most.

In the countryside there is no knowing whether the autumn colour is going to be particularly effective one year or not. There are so many factors that there is no foretelling, a long wet summer does not necessarily mean that there will not be good colour and conversely, a dry summer is no guarantee of colour. Leaves can fall too quick to let us enjoy the varied changing colours. However, though the same applies to the garden, there are some plants that can be relied on to produce a good show. The Virginia Creeper and the other vines will always turn brilliant shades of orange and red. The maples too can be relied on to paint themselves brightly. Some of the apple species and thorns are reliable, and these are mentioned in the chapter in trees. The Rhus species will all turn red, *Ribes americanum* will turn gold and red, and many species of Berberis are most effective. *B. thunbergii,* wilsonae and *yunnanense* all turn deep rich reds.

Where foliage is accompanied by fruit there is a chance that when leaves are dropped the colour of the fruit is still left behind and will take up well into the winter months. So it is with many *Malus* species, with *Berberis* species and hybrids, and with many *Contoneasters.* Some plants will drop only a proportion of their leaves, like *Berberis calliantha* so that here the green evergreen leaves are shining next to brilliant red ones,

TYPES OF DAHLIAS

SMALL
DECORATIVE

CHARM

CACTUS

LARGE
PAEONY

STAR

POMPOM

COLLARETTE

88

SINGLE

s Serrulata Shogetsu

A town garden in Chelsea

Cotoneaster horizontalis will lose its leaves over a long period often so that in general effect the leaves and berries are one.

And then back to winter when we look to the winter flowering shrubs and plants to brighten our days and to the evergreens and the bark of deciduous shrubs and trees.

Chapter 6

Do you take this tree . . . ?

Planting a tree is an act of faith. One thinks not of the immediate present but hopes for long life to enjoy the maturing tree with its crops of fruit or blossom. Most of us planting trees nowadays are still likely to use the young nursery grown stock and not the already mature or nearly mature trees that can be lifted, moved and replanted nowadays with comparative ease if one can foot the bill.

Choosing trees for the smaller garden presents problems. Obviously forest trees are not likely to prove a success, they are going to outgrow their home and maybe create friction with neighbours if given their heads. Nothing looks worse than the barbarous surgery that is resorted to on such occasions.

We need a smaller sized tree and one which will come to maturity fairly soon. Fortunately there is a good selection to choose from. One wonders whether it may not be possible in some future age for even some of the larger types to be grown on dwarfing rootstocks like fruit trees so that we can get semi-transistorised oaks and beeches for our back gardens. Of course some trees are very slow growing and remain within sensible bounds for as many years as we are likely to be interested in their behaviour. Such a one is the Strawberry Tree, *Arbutus unedo*, that is hardy in the warmer parts of the country. It might be more a shrub than a tree for many years. Other trees are strong growing brutes that benefit from surgery and can thereby be kept to the size ordained by the almighty saw handling gardener. Such are some of the willows whose pollarded growths will burst into activity with far reaching shooting stems whose coloured bark delights in winter. But some others are neither playing their part in juvenile years, nor are being cut to size, but are born to play the part.

We take them in alphabetical order, trying to weigh our comments to commend those that seem especially fit for the small garden but equally to point out the possible weaknesses. I think we should look if possible for a tree that makes a good shape and looks interesting at all times and that, although floral display does enter the points scale, not too much should be allowed for this alone.

Arbutus unedo

The Strawberry Tree is perhaps best treated as a shrub for it will take many years to attain its upward limit of perhaps fifteen, twenty or even thirty feet. It is an evergreen and a member of the heather family but it is one that does not mind lime in the soil. It forms a cumulus cloud shaped tree, a wide topped one. Its masses of dark shining green leather tough leaves make it a useful background for lighter coloured plants. It does have its unusual flowering time to commend it, blooming in the months from October till Christmas and having with its blossom the strawberry fruits resulting from last year's bloom. The shape of the white or pink tinted flowers show the plant's

91

allegiance to the heathers, for they are individually the same almost closed pitcher form.

Betula

The birches are a graceful set of trees, but it is doubtful if any species from America or Asia is more pleasing than our native *B. verrucosa*. Our Silver Birch has as fine a silver white trunk as any and can hardly be challenged in the delicacy of the patterns it weaves with graceful twigs and branches. A single tree looks well but even better is a group of three if space can be allowed. Planted closely for trees, just a few yards apart the three will form together a most satisfying picture. Alternatively one should look for the tree that has had its leader broken low down and now has two three or more competing branches reaching upwards and so performing a continuing silent play through each month of the year. The silver Birch is one of the easiest of trees to manage for it does well on even the poorest of soil. If you can get a good specimen or specimens with plenty of roots securely balled up in soil then they will probably grow away quickly and well. Trying to bring one home from the woods is likely to be a fruitless endeavour as well as a felonous one.

I do not know any tree that grows quicker from seed than some of these birches. A tiny seedling will put on several feet in a year. We had batches of *B. mandshurica* the Japanese White Birch, and *B. maximowicziana* which just seemed to rocket skywards in a few months. But I would stick with our native *B. verrucosa* or with *B. papyrifera* for its very white bark. *B.*

papyrifera may keep its white colouring into greater age than our native but it lacks something of the grace of the Silver Birch. There are of course many variants of the Silver Birch, quite a number of pendulous ones. Of these *B. v. pendula youngii* is probably the best with its very thin long branches hanging attractively. This tree is just the size most small gardens can cope with and the pendulous effect is light and attractive. It is in fact in this form a more suitable tree than the more widely planted weeping willows which I love dearly but which can grow quite large and produce too dense a mass of foliage for the smaller garden. In *Betula verrucosa pendula youngii* we have a winner; a pity we have not a brighter shorter name for it, even 'Young's Weeping Birch' scarsely has a zippy sound that would help sales.

Crataegus The Thorns.
The thorns are a formidable family in more ways than one Many are well armed physically, but the family is so numerous and relationships so intricate that it almost defies the efforts of botanists. Many thorns are most attractive trees of medium height and are definite character trees, just the thing for the small garden. Their only possible disadvantage is their slightly slow rate of growth. Here once again we might advocate planting a group of three trees to gain some quick effect, but with the idea of cutting out two of the three as soon as a single tree makes a decent specimen. Alternatively, a single tree can be flanked by shrubs that will provide interest and form whilst the tree gains stature. From the many hundreds of thorns that

have been named and described the short-listed ones are treated alphabetically.

arnoldiana. This is a fairly typical thorn, one of the newer described species, a tree of some fifteen to twenty-five feet high with a mass of widely angled branches heavily armed with thorns, some up to three inches long. The foliage is more or less oval but toothed and somewhat lobed. The tree produces generous crops of wide white clusters of flowers which are followed by bright red berries. These berries do not last as long into the winter as some other thorns which may be preferred on this count alone.

x *carrierei*. This hybrid is a robust sturdy tree of some fifteen to twenty feet high handsomely clothed with shiny rich green foliage. In June it decks itself out with many wide bunches of white flowers. The fruits that follow are orange red speckled brown and these hang decoratively on the branches through the winter. So at no season is the tree without its appeal.

crus-gallii. Cockspur Thorn. This well known thorn is one of the most indestructible of trees and will remain an ornament in a garden decades after some of the Cherries have passed their prime and broken down. It is usually a tree of some twenty feet in maturity though it can be more. It forms a wide topped dome of a mushroom or umbrella outline. This shape makes it one of the most distinctive of thorns and in the running for one of the outstanding tree silhouettes of all. The form makes it a natural for the gardener looking for something different, but it is of course a prolific bloomer smothering itself with white blossom, and then with autumn its foliage turns rich shades of orange and red so emphasising its role as a focal point and not to lose its audience it retains crops of deep red fruit from October right through the winter. Of course it must have thorns, these measure up to three inches but can be longer still.

x *grignonensis.* This hybrid probably has the last mentioned species as one parent and has some of its good qualities. It makes a tree of similar height, with heavy crops of red fruits that shine brightly through the winter. It tends to keep its leaves rather later than most.

oxyacantha coccinea plena. 'Pauls Double Scarlet'. This is a well known tree. Here is the common hawthorn in party dress. A mature gnarled old hawthorn is an impressive tree. This sport can naturally have all the points of its parent, but it is a very fine flowering form, for all the flowers are a rich crimson with a pinky tinge and the doubled effect of the flowers does tend to make the floral display last longer.

orientalis. This is another medium sized tree with spreading branches that form a wide topped somewhat rounded tree of pleasing form. The branches tend to fall in a lightly pendulous way, gently, a suggestion rather than a full blooded statement of intent. It is a beautiful medium sized tree. It looks well with its clothing of dark green foliage, it looks attractive in bloom, it charms with its crops of orange or red fruits.

persistens. Hardly a romantic name, but it does give us the clue to some part of the character of this small but pleasing tree. It is a typical armed thorn, a wide spreading one of modest height maybe only 12 or so feet. The persistens part of its character relates to the dark clothes, for the shining fresh foliage is dropped only late, well into November, and the crop of fruits lasts through the winter in its dark rather dull red tones. It is thought that it may be a hybrid of our old friend the Cockspur Thorn.

punctata. A tree usually satisfied to reach twenty feet but measuring more in width. This is one of the best thorns for its display of blossom, having very many wide clusters of white flowers in June. It carries a crop of red fruits spotted darker.

tomentosa. Here is another tree of modest height, perhaps only fifteen feet but may be another five foot with age or in good conditions. It is a tree of character, its branches often twisting into interesting patterns. It looks very well in blossom for it is generous with its flower, but its other festive time is in the autumn when the foliage lights up into rich carnival colours of orange and red. The fruit is less darkly coloured than most, being an orange gold.

Cytisus battandierii

What you may ask is what are we doing with a cytisus listed amongst trees? This broom is one on its own and though we must own that it is a shrub, it does have some of the stature of a small tree in the proportions that we are dealing with in this book. *C. battandierii* grows to some fifteen feet and it gets there rapidly for it has plenty of that quick maturing energy of the genus. It has been thought tender, and perhaps we cannot mark it down as the shrub most likely to survive a new Ice Age but we had it growing happily in Northumberland as well as in the south. It is certainly worth a place in the garden for its foliage is bold and quite vividly silvered. Each leaf is about three inches long so that the whole effect of the strongly growing upward reaching bush-cum-tree is light and a refreshing contrast especially if planted in the sun against some dark leaved shrub like holly. Its floral productions are quite happy affairs in rich gold, a rather tight bunch of peaflowers that may be variously scented often curiously like pineapple, in fact the flower bunches are so restricted that they have the general appearance of fruits. Like all of its family it is most quickly grown from seed.

Laburnums

The laburnums are botanically close relatives of the broom family and are as easy to grow, as witness the thousands that delight us every May and June festooning themselves with such an amount of golden blossom as to seem almost overdoing a good thing. The size of the trees make them particularly suitable for the small garden, for they are usually content with a height of twenty feet though they can go another ten on occassions. They are trees that come early into maturity and so give us a quota of blossom from their earliest years. They are likewise not the longest lived of species and the cutting of branches of established trees will often hasten their death. I think few trees look better in groups, even if for the sake of space they should be squashed rather close to each other. The larger gardens can afford the room to plant maybe a dozen and really have a feast, we must content ourselves with say three or even a single specimen, and if it is to be a single one let us start with a bush shape and allow several

FLOWERING TREES

PRUNUS · FLOWERING CHERRY

SYRINGA · LILAC

LABURNUM

MAGNOLIA

leaders to go upwards from a foot or two above soil level.

The laburnums are a small family. The common one, *L. anagyroides*, will often branch low from the ground unless the nurseryman has been watching it and obliging it to be single minded. The blossom is too well known to need description, the golden rain makes the tree a deluging cloud. The Scotch Laburnum. *L. alpinum* is maybe the better of the two. It opens a week or two later but the golden racemens are even longer and more graceful. There are a number of hybrids between these two species. Two very similar kinds are listed as L. x watererii and L. x vossii. They are excellent trees with conspicuously long racemes of flowers.

Though I am always interested in oddities I do not make a collection of them in my garden. Therefore I do not have the Purple Laburnum *Laburno Cytis x adamu*, but tastes vary and this is certainly a most interesting tree. It was derived from the grafting of the purple broom, *C. purpureus*, onto the stock of the common laburnum. This original graft was made as long ago as 1825. The flower racemes are six or so inches long and a yellow heavily mingled with purple. But the plant often betrays its parentage by having odd branches of the pure laburnum and also the purple broom, so that one can find at one and the same time three types of flowers on the tree, the most curious part being where the pure broom character has asserted itself for here we find the typical broom growth, the thick mass of green twigs like a witch's broom.

Magnolia
This fine family of shrubs and trees scarcely owns a poor one.

Some we must exclude for growing too tall and for taking too long about reaching sufficient maturity to give of their best florally. Others like *M. stellata* are obviously shrubs. Some of the most reliable and garden worthy do not clearly fall into shrub or tree category easily. They grow from one to the other with age. So, abandoning for the present our usual alphabetical method, we take the most popular of all magnolias, *M. soulangiana,* This is a hybrid and has several forms. It comes from the fine *M. denudata* but, as it makes a more pleasingly shaped tree and grows more quickly, we shall pay mother homage and praise the daughter. *M. soulangiana* forms a rather low but wide spreading tree with upward reaching branches. The branches are not produced with such freedom as to produce a dense effect. Indeed one gains the impression in April that the shrub or tree has been arranged as a candelabrum to hold the large flowers to their very best advantage. The flowers in April are borne on the bare branches but they continue to open through May till into June when the leaves are unfurled. The large flowers are white within and are more or less stained purple outside. Some forms are quite conspicuously purpled, but all are fine things.

Many of the other magnolias are somewhat less hardy and are seen at their best in the southwest, but the warm influence of a nearby wall can work wonders. *M. wilsonii* is a shrub or small tree that is usually quite hardy unless planted in a most exposed position. Grown into a small tree it is most pleasing for the flowers are hung looking downwards, set like lights through the tree. They open in June against the background

100

of the young green foliage, the white cups made to look purer by the dark red central boss formed of the many stamens.

Both the two species mentioned above are deciduous, the noble *M. grandiflora* is an evergreen. A tree that can reach sixty or more feet high might be thought somewhat out of the scale of things we are considering, but by planting a young specimen it is unlikely that the gardener will have a great deal of interest in the tree by the time it reaches these exalted heights. It is no magic beanstalk, though once settled it makes, in the schoolmaster's phrase, 'steady progress.' Though the tree is hardy, it benefits in most parts from the protection of a wall and this can afford a means of holding the branches that can be tragically broken by heavy falls of snow such as we have experienced during the past few winters. It may well be that the influence of the wall will be felt in helping the tree to come into a flowering disposition earlier and on this score it is well to note that of the varieties that one can purchase it is the 'Exmouth' one which seems to have the habit of earlier flowering. The flowers are of course magnificent, the finest of a fine genus, great thick petalled globes that can be anything from six to close on twelve inches across. It may also be mentioned that this 'Exmouth' kind, sometimes listed as *M. g. lanceolata* on account of its somewhat narrower leaves, is of a more upright build and therefore ideally suited to wall cultivation. The flowers have a spicy smell. It would be no bad thing to advise planting this as a wall shrub or tree on account of its foliage alone for its evergreen is in the simple satisfying bold design as the common laurel, but it is best out of the wildest winds.

101

Malus

The apples are a large race, and large numbers of them are suitable for the smaller garden. As a race they are long-lived, but, unlike some families where this is true, they do not have the frustrating habit of taking many years before flowering and fruiting. In the garden the natural competitors of the apple species and hybrids are the flowering Cherries and one would have to be a horticultural Solomon to decide which has the greater claim to our allegiance and favour for a position in the garden. There is no doubting that some cherries in full bloom are a perfect miracle. The clouds of blossom convert the well known plot into a wonderland. Many come to perform another act in the autumn when their foliage turns golden, orange and red. But the apples are scarcely less profuse in their blossoming, and many hang their branches with bright gay fruit for many weeks through autumn and winter months. Some kinds might be thought to form trees or bushes of more pleasing shape than some of the cherries. We can mention only a few now.

If we stand in need of a dark leaved small tree, something to give the dramatic effect of a copper beech, but scaled down to manageable size, we might well consider one of the purple leaved apples and our choice might well rest with *M. lemoinei.* This is one of a number of hybrids, it has dark trunk, stems, and deep purple leaves. It does have a good show of dark red single flowers in the spring.

Malus spectabilis flore pleno is a crab apple that may grow ultimately to the height of the house but it takes its time, and each spring it can stand comparison with any of its kin, for it dresses itself over all with very doubled 2 inch flowers that are a pleasing rosy red in bud but open to a smiling blush shade. It is a trick of many of the apples, tight lipped buds are heavily roughed, the open smiling faces are delicate shades of pink. *'Hillierii'* is one such. It blooms profusely but has bud and open flower together for a period when the pattern of colour is at its most delightful. Its foliage is standard green. *M. sargentii* also plays the game, but in this the pink buds become pure white. It is a shrub of modest stature perhaps happy with some eight feet headroom, but it is usually sold in the form of a small standard and as such can be sited in even the smallest garden. Certainly here one would note the fragrance of the bloom, enjoy the green leaves turining to gold and orange with autumn, and count the weeks as the many but quite tiny dark red fruits swing long-stalked from the branches through September and October probably into November.

The crab apple proper is *M. pumila,* and of this character there are many forms. Who would not love to be able to transport some old and gnarled specimen to sit in its ancient glory like a piece of fantastic sculpture in our garden. For the gnarled old specimen most of us must wait wondering whether tree or tree-lover will be most gnarled first. Of the crab varieties the favourite is probably 'John Downie'. It has the qualities we need. The foliage is a good healthy deep green, the flowers in pink babyhood open to single white winged beauty, individually larger than most. In autumn it tests the muscles of its branches by ladening them with magnificent crops of orange red fruits.

But we are spoilt with apples, there are too many good ones.

For early red blossom we might have 'Liset' with its large single flowers, its purple foliage, and crops of purple red fruits. We might plant 'Gorgeous' rejoicing in its display of blossom so typically apple blossom coloured. Certainly, if we are picturing the fruiting display in the back end, we cannot afford to dismiss this fine kind, for the fruit is abundant and beautiful in its rich red and it stays tied to the tree until we begin to buy and post Christmas cards. It plays the role of 'Cheals Crimson' or the 'Red Siberian Crab' but it plays even these fine actors off the stage. A happy change of colour can be enjoyed in these dreary autumn and winter months by the display of 'Golden Hornet' with its bunches, masses of shining golden fruits. Here again we have a pink budded floral beauty that opens pure white innocence against the young green foliage.

Prunus

I would bring the government down over the matter of these cherries if I could, or rather over such lunacy as must lie behind defence expenditure or supersonic aircraft. No need to protest about precious acres being squandered on huge sounding boards of airfields. Cherry lovers of the kingdom unite! Let us slice off just a tiny percentage from government expenditure and finding some county or centre unfavoured by a Stratford tourist attraction plant its acres with cherries by the hundreds, the thousands and the tens of thousands. The tourists will come, even if we do not allow supersonic flight, they will certainly come, for cherries in a mass are miraculous. All gardeners must have a sense of wonder, but all with eyes, gardeners or not, must pause to gaze at the cherry in blossom. Where one day the bare branches cut grey shapes out of the sky, on the next the sap has risen and assaulted every part so that the smallest twig transcends material earth and becomes a flligree miracle of beauty, a cloud scarcely rooted to earth, a dream of beauty undefiled, a silent symphony of magic from unknown dimensions, the pure breath of creation. Has God created a finer tree than a cherry?

Where beauty is crowded by beauty how may one be chosen and the rest left? It is no new problem to the gardener and, as life is merely the continuing opportunity of choice, we exercise our minds and spirit in picking a few cherries, starting not with the species which seems normal good manners in horticultural writing, but with the hybrid garden cherries for which we may thank the dedicated work of many generations of Japanese flower lovers.

Yes, we have to start with 'Kanzan,' whether it is planted under this name or as 'Sekiyama' or 'Hi-Zakura' or any of its several synomens. This is the tree that has been so widely planted and which so fantastically loads itself with large double deep pink flowers. There is no doubt that this must be one of the most floriferous of trees and it deserves its popularit , it has the same happy generosity as the forsythias with their golden blossom and it grows with similar vigorous temperament. If one must find fault, then it is a tendency for the tree to send its branches too rigidly upright poking too vulgarly heavenwards like an umbrella cruelly blown inside out. But this tendency can be corrected in youth by pruning, cutting back

105

the few main branches once, and yet again later, to an outside facing bud. Again, if we are going to make a meal of aesthetics, we might feel that 'Kanzan,' loving display, has thrown wisdom to the wind and loved too well. Can it be so? I believe our Japanese friends would smile politely at the floral meals we allow ourselves with this, they would choose some of the single flowered kinds perhaps. Are we going to be puritan and deny ourselves or shall be have a real feast.

The young foliage of 'Kanzan' is a bright coppery colour. 'Pink Perfection' is hardly so bright in its young leaves and has not quite the same amount of pigment in its flowers, but it certainly has the same reckless abandonment to ornament in flower and these are again very large. It may be added that it makes perhaps a rather better shaped tree more easily. 'Fugenzo' is another fine cherry in this colouring and general character. It opens rather later than 'Kanzan' and will have flowers and leaves intermingling, the effect made apparently more noticeable by its habit of forming two or three green carpels in the wide open flowers. The rich pink blossom and young coppery foliage make a fine picture on the wide spreading pattern of branches that make a broad topped tree of quite low height.

In paler shades the variety 'Hokusai' forms a widespread tree that decks itself out with garlands of cheerful bright but paler pink flowers than the previous mentioned kinds. It is none the worse for that and may for this very reason melt more satisfyingly into the garden design than the darker pinks. Counted flower by flower, there are as many a million on this tree as any

106

other kind.

Kiku Shidare Zakura' is one name of many that this cherry is known as, it is however a distinct kind which can be perhaps more easily identified as the 'Oriental Weeping Cherry' once it is made certain that one is not talking about the pendulous forms of *P. subhirtella*. It has the attraction of all hanging or weeping trees and is well hung with deep rose coloured very double flowers. It is a dramatic tree in silhouette, so strongly pendant, and on this account can be both useful in the right position or artificially histrionic in the wrong place. It is an actor for the deliberate gesture and is not going to melt into a more natural decor.

Following our weeping actor we might well turn to a couple of cherries that exaggerate the opposite gesture. Flinging arms rigidly upwards 'Amanogawa' poses as a column and as such a piece of architecture one may use it. Its branches are closely clustered in this narrow upright form which must seem un-natural and tiresome if the cherry is overplanted, but one plant or a group of three can be effective, explosive punctuation in garden composition. The thick bunches of powder pink blossoms are secured to each twig and branch end in carnival spirit. *P. hillierii* 'Spire' acts this same role and puts on its party dress of pink flowers very early in the year.

So far we have mentioned only the pink flowered kinds, but the white cherries maybe have a purer, even more wonderful etherial beauty. True some like 'Shirofugen' open double and pink and attain whiteness, as does the lovely 'Shogetsu,' but some are born white and remain white. Of course the cherry that grows wild in our countryside is no mean beauty, and, in its double form, it is a tree of outstanding beauty and of such character as to warrant planting in parks, roadsides and where ever we want to add generous beauty to the country-side in trees of strong growth and quite noble form. *P. avium plena* is likely to be too big for the small garden though it could have many flowering seasons before it pushed its territorial claims into disputed areas. Where the double pink 'Kanzan' swirls its dress, there we might have planted another cherry of similar size but of very different character. 'Tai Haku' is distinguished by having the largest flowers of any cherry, and if this sounds as if we are talking of a gross horticultural freak do not worry. Large the flowers may be, but they are single and of gentle somewhat lacy outline, gracefully hung on quite long stalks so that their beauty can be the better appreciated as it contrasts with the bronze and red copper that overlays the young green of the leaves. The tree is strong.

Of course the *Prunus* family is crowded with good things apart from cherries, for there are the almonds, the peaches, apricots, plums and laurels. *P. amygdalopersica* or as it is perhaps more correctly known *P. communis* is the Almond that explodes in a pink cloud in March. It is the right size for us at some ten to twenty feet and though there are several named forms including double ones, none is better than what is usually planted as the type plant. It does perhaps lack a little in grace when out of bloom. *P. subhirtella autumnalis* with somewhat pendulous smaller branches arching downwards from the wide angled wide spreading larger main branches is perhaps a more pleasing shape. Although its flowers are small it does produce them at a time when there is little blossom. Depending on the weather it will bloom once, twice, or in several flurries like the light advanced powdering falls of snow that often come before the real fall. The flowers usually come after the leaves have been lost any time from October through the winter months and often again as the leaves are beginning to free themselves from their small tight buds.

Perhaps at its best as a shrub, *P. incisa* is a delightful plant, the moderately sized flowers being freely borne over the naked wood, as shower of white given a pink cast sometimes by the rich colour of the calyx. Wide open frank flowers delicately strung on their branches have an immediate appeal. By training it can be formed into a modestly sized tree of rather rounded form. It has the natural grace of the wildling. In contrast the *P. cerasifera nigra,* or *P. cerasifera pissardii nigra,* the Purple Leaved Plum seems to me to be a tree of very plebeian character and if one wants purple foliage I think there are more pleasing trees of this colour to be found in other genera. But of course it is a matter of opinion. What I would suggest is that only the odd tree with purple foliage should be allowed guest room. A touch of garlic can bring the taste buds into active life, more than a touch and the whole is a depressing drowned disaster, and so it is with the purple leaved plants. One may be a stimulant, more than one and the depressent effect is felt.

Salix

I am fond of willows whether they weep, creep, twist or fasciate themselves. In the small garden the tree sized willows must be chosen carefully, the golden weeping willow so commonly seen planted can outgrow a small plot surprisingly quickly. If one plants one it may be kept in some sort of check by the skilful use of secateurs and saw. The thing to do is never to allow the tree to get too big. However it may be thought wiser to leave this and the traditional weeping willow, *S. babylonica*, to those who have the room. A small weeping tree can be purchased under the name *S. purpurea pendula*. A pendulous form of the species is grafted on stems some eight to ten feet high and so form a fountain head of many thin branches clothed with thin leaves. I like it.

Though at their natural heights quite out of the question for the small garden the species normally grown for their coloured bark can be kept just as tall as you want and within reason the more they are cut back the more vigorous and more effective the new growths become. *S. alba chermesina* has orange yellow, bark, and *S. daphnoides* has purple stems more or less covered with a white bloom. This bark looks well in the winter garden and can even be used with good effect as cut twigs indoors. Another willow that the flower arranger will be attacking is *S. matsudana tortuosa*. Called the 'Hancow Corkscrew Tree,' this rapidly growing willow spirals its way upward to form a pleasantly formed tree of graceful form. Effective all year round with its twisting stems and curly leaves, it is perhaps at its best in the winter when its contortions can be seen most clearly and the jig saw patterns it cuts out of the sky can be most appreciated. Though it will in many years form a largish tree, this will take a long time and its size can be kept in check.

Sorbus

The wild rowans or mountain ashs are one of our most lovely character trees set in the wilder parts of our landscape. In the garden too the huge crops of berries can shine brightly for many weeks. It takes a little time to form a wide enough trunk to give the tree its character and for my money the ones that branch low down and have more than one straight trunk look far better. A group of three looks well. Of course now there are very many named hybrid Sorbus with wonderful coloured fruits. They look most effective. One can take a choice from many such as 'Apricot Queen,' 'Brilliant Yellow,' 'Chemois Glowing Pink,' 'Copper Glow,' 'Lombarts Golden Wonder,' 'Maiden-blush,' 'Pink Queen,' 'Salmon Queen,' 'Vermilion,' and 'White Wax.'

The Sorbus family of course includes the Whitebeams, quick growing healthy looking trees of good symmetrial pyramidical form. *S. edules majestica* has good broad tough dark green foliage with the typical silver white undersurface, the leaves being larger than others whilst the bunches of berries are a rich shining red.

If I had been born in some other age, a savage in some wild jungle, I would have been happy to sit down and worship a tree. We must plant trees.

Chapter 7

The Answer is Shrubs

The solution the gardener aims for is maximum effect; effect from plants that personally please the most. Into the equation go the familiar factors, time, energy, space, and cost. Some forms of gardening are handicapped for their high t,e,s, and c ratings. Large scale bedding plans that demand a continual succession of rainbow effects have normally to be left to the public parks. Large scale rock gardens become sparse; flat, or almost flat rock beds taking their place. The herbaceous border becomes less herbaceous and more shrubby. Whatever happened to topiary?

Of course new techniques and new discoveries alter the balance of the equation at times. Some prophets foretell a return to bedding schemes and annual borders. They believe we shall buy our garden borders in rolls of papers or material, unrolling the chosen 'Chelsea Extra' design (15 feet by 6 feet of riotous technicolor for only 19/11d)" onto the border, pegging it down at intervals (plastic pegs in envelope 1), water the lot (automatically from a button fifteen inches to the righthand side of the armchair), and await the results No weeds are present due to the chemical impregnated in the roll, clear of the flower seeds. This inhibits the germination of weed seeds. Certainly at present experiments are taking place, and have been

112

for a while, under the auspices of big chemical interests both with a view to establishing the kinds of garden plants most resistant to certain herbicides or germination inhibiting sprays. The idea is to recommend planting schemes for borders that thereafter may be kept entirely weed-free by watering all over with a chemical spray every other month or so.

At present one of the most attractive things that may be said about a plant is that it is labour saving. Shrubs lead the labour saving brigade. Having been planted, most require little or no looking after and by their shade they help to smother or inhibit any weed growth. The varying forms, foliage, and architecture of branches gives depth to the garden picture at all times, not only for a few weeks of floral display but throughout the year. Not that flowers need be in very short supply for long around the year, the winter flowers being augmented by crops of berries and coloured bark.

These then are the shrubs that I would choose to have in my ideal garden, omitting the roses mentioned in another chapter. In a book this size no possible claim for completeness can be put forward, the selection is of ones I find attractive.

Berberis

This large clan of craggy individualists is to most a bewildering botanical jungle, the very size of the family tending to make it less popular than others and than it deserves. The thorny armour perhaps hinders popularity as well. In one of our gardens we built up quite a representative collection of these species. We found out after we moved that the new owner had cleared every last one and planted the cleared space with bedding plants and a monkey puzzle tree. I rather fancy he might have found the bedding plants a lot more trouble to look after. Certainly, in more pagan moments I have wished that the berberis bushes gave a good account of themselves before they went their way to glory.

The following are some that I find handsome, distinctive, or just plain likeable.

beaniana 8 feet June China

A crowded upright deciduous shrub that then arches at the top and can hang itself with multitudes of bright purple berries in bunches. At this stage in the late summer, autumn and early winter it is at its most showy. The dark foliage is more or less toothed, each leaf measuring from one to two inches and a quarter the width. Flowers are deep yellow cups a quarter of an inch deep.

brachypoda 8 feet May China

Young leaves, shoots, and thorns of this one are downy, most unusual for a Berberis. The leaves are especially downy below. It is deciduous with oval leaves up to three inches long, sometimes well toothed but sometimes clean cut. It gained an Award of Merit when shown in fruit. The fruits are oval, close to half an inch long, and borne in thick hanging clusters of rich deep red. Flowers are pale primrose.

calliantha 2-3 feet May Tibet.

This is a low growing evergreen which will grow several times wider than high. It forms a mass of highly polished holly like foliage of rich green. A proportion of these leaves will be lost each year and these take of a rich red colour before falling. Whilst, like many of the family, the underneath surface of the leaves is not readily noticed, this is conspicuously silvered. The pale yellow flowers are perhaps an inch across, carried 1, 2 or 3 at a time to make a quiet and dignified rather than a spectacular display. Berries are nearly black with a plum like bloom.

candidula 4 feet May China

This is a densely growing dwarf shrub which may well content itself with slowly producing a rounded bush about three feet high. The leaves are very narrow and a dark green though a surprising blue white below. Flowers are quite large for a berberis, over half an inch across, a shining yellow, but are borne only singly to be followed in due course by oval purple tiny plums about $\frac{1}{2}$-inch long.

concinna 3 feet June Himalaya

This is a pleasant dwarf with shining green leaves most strikingly white on the under surfaces. They are about an inch long and toothed. Half inch flowers are carried singly and followed by rather luscious looking oblong red berries, some nearly half an inch long.

darwinii 15 feet May Chile

This well known species has been grown here for over a century. Some long established specimens are over 15 feet but many more ordinary mature specimens will be 6 to 12 feet high. It is a densely growing evergreen with tiny holly leaves of very dark glossy green that makes all the more effective the display of bloom through May and June. Then the bush catches fire. Flaming bunches of hanging golden and orange flowers light up the bush. Often tinged with red, the blossom is most beautiful. As an extra dividend the bush can look quite distinguished later with a display of dark blue berries.

hakeoides 8 feet May Chile.

I enjoy the unusual provided it is not just a freak. This shrub I find a totally acceptable nonconformist individual. It is evergreen and a rangey beast capable of exceptionally vigorous growth. It sends stems upright for several feet into the air with scarcely any branching. The pairs of leaves along this length may vary from half to three inches long. At the base they are attached by stalks perhaps $1\frac{1}{2}$-2 feet long, but the nearer they approach the top the shorter the stalks become so that eventually the leaves cling around the stem but are held boldly at 45° up to right angles with it. These leaves are thick and strong, like leather, and are broad in a basically circular or heart shaped form with well formed spiny teeth. The tough foliage and spines make one rejoice for a real individualist, but the floral display is not altogether negligible. It produces bunches of quite large individual flowers from the leaf axils of last year's wood.

jamesiana 10 feet May China

This is an Award of Merit species. It gained this for its heavy crops of berries that hang glistening and translucent like clusters of Red Currants. The scarlet fruits are round and nearly $\frac{1}{2}$ inch across. The foliage, only rarely or lightly, toothed, is rather prominently mesh veined. Before the foliage falls it turns a good red so that with the scarlet fruits the shrubs can provide a fine spectacle in September, October and November.

julianae 10 feet May China

116

A robust species, that looks healthy enough to feature in a fertilizer advertisement. It produces an opulent mound of rich green foliage, dense, intricate, thorny, and unyielding as the commissioners for inland revenue. Perhaps it earns the prize as the hardiest of the berberises. It builds itself up to 20 feet or so, and, with middle-age spread, rather more through. It arms itself with three-way spines that can be two inches long, and clothes itself with evergreen narrow teethed foliage. Yellow flowers are carried in clusters, the fruit is oval, and very dark with a blue bloom.

linearifolia 9 feet April Chile

One of the best of the family, an evergreen that at any height between four and nine feet may be at the maximum for the individual's performance. The sharp pointed narrow dark leaves contrast well with the clusters of cup-shaped salmon flowers that are orange inside. They are over half an inch across and are amongst the richest coloured of the genus.

montana 16 feet May S. America

This is a vigorous deciduous barberry of graceful form particularly pleasing in May when the large flowers of gold and tangerine are hung out in decorative profusion. Individual flowers may be close to an inch across, giant size for a berberis. The branches are fortified with three pronged spines but the leaves are clean cut. The berries are black with a dark bloom.

morrisonensis 8 feet June Formosa

A deciduous species at its best before leaf fall when the foliage is painted a cheerful mixture of all kinds of gold, orange and scarlet and the branches are hung with bunches of rich red globes close to half an inch long and shining in semi-translucent manner. The new shoots are red in Spring, the flowers are pale yellow.

replicata 5 feet March-May China

This pleasant evergreen with very narrow dark unpolished foliage has rather slender arching branches. It will open its clusters of golden flowers early in the spring. Its fruit crop is of longish red berries that eventually become black.

x *rubrostilla* wilsonae x aggregata

This hybrid is one of the things for which we may thank the R.H.S. Gardens at Wisley. It was raised there and was given a First Class Certificate during the First World War. Quite a crowd of other hybrids have come from this or similar parentage. All are most lovely in the autumn when they carry heavy crops of berries attractively arranged slung along their wide reaching stems. These berries are beautiful shades of red, pink and orange made all the more attractive by their luscious translucent quality. A selection of seedlings might be grown in a group to harmonize and complement each other. One of my favourites is 'Cherry Ripe' with berries coloured delightful shades of coral pink at their best stage. This shrub with wide arching stems, like the others of the group, has neat smallish leaves that also take a part in the colourful autumn display.

stenophylla 10 feet April May darwinii x empetrifolia.

I included *B. darwinii* in my list, but if shipwrecked on a desert island with only room for one, stenophylla would have to be the chosen one. It forms a thicket, solid with stems and spine tipped leaves. From the mass are thrown arching rods, that,

THE ANSWER IS SHRUBS

after a year, are strewn with small golden flowers, each small in itself, but in such quantity that the effect is delightful. The berries are plum coloured with white bloom.

wilsonae 6 feet May China

One of the parents of x *rubrostilla* and with the same charm as the hybrids. It is a neat spreading bush most pretty when hung with large crops of coral translucent berries. More or less deciduous.

yunnanensis 6 feet May China

This is a deciduous species of thick rounded form. With primrose flowers $\frac{3}{4}$-inch across, leaves up to $1\frac{1}{2}$-inches long, 1 inch spines, and oval berries at least $\frac{1}{2}$-inch long this is one of the most favoured of species. It is most spectacular when the autumn paints the foliage in vivid dark reds.

Cotoneasters

I do not think there can be another family easier to grow or less trouble to look after. We have grown many from seed and find them quick to establish themselves and make nice plants.

adpressa $1\frac{1}{2}$ feet May China

A sufferer from vertigo that hugs the ground or rocks by which it is planted. Inflexible branches form a thick flat pattern hump-backed over the ground. The rather dull dark green leaves are joined in Spring by the unspectacular flowers of white tinged pink and at this time these may be obscured by the bees and other visitors that can make these cotoneasters hum like a generator. The round berries are red. A useful rock garden plant.

bullata 15 feet China, Tibet

This shrub casts a few long rods in widespread form. Its foliage is of dark green leaves up to or more than three inches long and like felt below. These fall in autumn. The bunches of flowers are noticed as a token of good things to come, they open in succession and fall in as quick a succession. But in fruit the shrub comes into its own, with scarlet berries in 2-inch bunches strung thickly along the branches.

conspicua. 1 to 8 feet May Tibet

Some botanists viewing a plant are in danger of finding one species looking at it from the left and another when viewing from the right. Some of the work of the 'splitters' in other genera especially bulbous ones makes one almost despair, not that a wholsale 'lumper' is not almost as bad. The cotoneasters are a variable lot and doubtless some of the 'species' in our gardens are merely forms one of another, but perhaps having names that we recognise is a convenience when dealing with shrubs. Of *C. conspicua* there are at least two distinct forms grown. The commonly offered kind is a low growing plant. In this stiff jointed form, the very dark almost black evergreen foliage cover is lit up with a pleasant show of white blossom in May to be followed by a good crop of close-held polished scarlet berries. The other form is tall and erect growing.

x *cornubia* 20 feet May frigida x?

Long into the winter this wide spreading tall growing hybrid has terrific crops of vivid scarlet berries in big bunches. Like others of the large contoneasters it can be encouraged to form a small tree by restricting the young plant to one stem and removing the lower growths. The plant has more foliage than

owing the use of mixed planting in a North London garden

Ornamental garage runway

Vitis Coignetial in a London garden setting

many, rich green leaves some almost six inches long. The heaviest cropper of all.

dielsiana 8 feet June China

Long slender stems arching out and down form a widespread spraying fountain of branches, green leaves, and, in the autumn, scarlet berries. A graceful shrub and good grower.

divarcata 6 feet May China

This, like the last, is a graceful deciduous species. The leaves are broad and dark green, the egg shaped berries are vermilion and are strung like beads, two or three at a time, along the whipping branches.

frigida 20 feet May Himalayas

This large rounded deciduous shrub is often grown as a small tree and as such is one of the most useful ones for the smaller garden. It is a robust species much more densely branched than many of the other larger kinds. It will form a thicket perhaps 15 feet through in time, but by keeping the young bush to one growth it will form a grey trunk supporting a round head. The branches have large leaves, some up to nearly six inches long and two inches wide. Depending on the appetite of the local birds, the huge bunches of large crimson scarlet berries will shine from September till February.

henryana 12 feet May China

This is an evergreen distinguished by having the largest leaves of the evergreen kinds, from two to six inches long and less than half as wide. The few long branches arch out and down, most gracefully. Wide bunches of white flowers are opened in June and are followed by crimson fruit.

horizontalis 3 feet May China

Deservedly the most popular of the genus. The fish-bone design of its flat opposite branching stems, the low prostrate habit, the many neat little leaves with the often abundant crops of berries help to make this species one that might well be included in every garden. The shrub in flower can whirr and hum with bee life. In the autumn the leaves turn varying shades of orange and red and augment the good colour of the many small beads stuck over the close fish bone branches. It is a shrub of beauty and utility. It will clothe a bank, there keeping low over the ground. It will grow up against a wall, and can help mask what might be an unsightly garden shed or fence.

microphylla 3 feet June Himalayas

This is the well known low growing widespreading scrambling shrub with narrow angled branches well clothed with small dark grey-green leaves. The fruits are round, a rich pinky red with a rather unpolished finish. Perhaps its smaller relative *C. thymae-folia* is better in choicer parts of the garden but on banks and walls this can be useful.

rotundifolia 8 feet June Himalayas

This excellent shrub is rather like a larger *C. horizontalis,* somewhat more open but still of stiff form. It has many large red berries that decorate the plant in the autumn and through the winter often till the first daffodils begin to open. It will usually retain a good quota of its dark rounded leaves through the winter.

salicifolia 15 feet June China

A wide spreading vigorous shrub, more or less evergreen, with oval leaves from one to four inches long. The graceful branching habit, with its foliage and large bunches of pea sized shining scarlet berries make this a fine sight in autumn and winter.

serotina 10 feet July August China

This evergreen is quite handsome in bloom as it has large quantities of small white flowers, but its season is the winter when its red berries will outlast those of other species, still being hung on the branches in spring.

thymaefolia 1 foot June Himalayas

Like a smaller *C. microphylla* with neat polished evergreen foliage and bright red fruit. Produces many branches in intricate patterns.

watererii 20 feet June *C. henryana* x *C. frigida*

Undisciplined this is a fine shrub, with attention a pleasant small tree. More or less evergreen, this has leaves up to three inches long of dark green. Scarlet fruits are carried in 2-inch clusters.

Cytisus

A garden can be filled in two or three years from a few packets of seeds of this fast growing and prolifically blooming family. The ones I would choose to have would be the following but there are many other fine kinds.

albus 10 feet May Spain and Portugal

Seedlings grow with the fantastic precociousness of the family, becoming a lovely sight in as few as three years. It is a hardy broom with gushing quantities of white flowers all over last year's wood. It grows tall and perhaps a trifle thin below so that it is best grown in small groups between rhododendrons or other more densely clothed shrubs.

battandierii 15 to 20 feet June Morocco

Quite the most distinct of brooms, a Moroccan plant that was only introduced into this country in the early twenties. It has proved hardy; we have had it growing in Essex and Northumberland with equal success. It has very large attractive foliage, soft

SHRUBS

FORSYTHIA   CYTISUS · BROOM   WEIGELA

and silvered with fine silky hairs. Stems grow strongly forming branches reaching up to over 15 feet. The flowers of bright gold are carried in close bunches, rather like a longish cone. The fragrance is often like pineapples.

decumbens 6 inches May June S. Europe

Sweeping the soil, the first branches can only be an inch or so

124

high, later ones lie flat over the first, so adding a few inches to height whilst growing very widespread. Generous with its golden blossom.

demissus 4 inches May Greece

Slender shoots clothed with neat bright green foliage lies low on the ground. The golden flowers that freely decorate it take on a reddish glow as they age.

SHRUBS

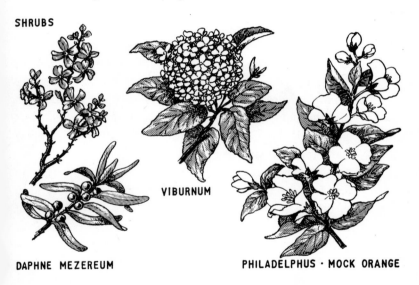

VIBURNUM

DAPHNE MEZEREUM   PHILADELPHUS · MOCK ORANGE

x *kewensis* 1 foot May *C. ardonnii* x *C. albus*

This famous hybrid is one of my chief favourites in a most likeable genus. It is excellent in the large rock garden or on a sunny bank where, though only reaching a foot high, it will go eight times as far horizontally. But it can be grown anywhere in the sun. The whole becomes a bubbling frothy mass of creamy white and palest sulphur for weeks in spring.

Daphne mezereum 3 feet winter

To my mind the daphnes are a very mixed lot. Some I enjoy with reservations, others are enjoyable in bloom but are scarcely distinguished in growth, and others are not worth growing. The commonest grown, *D. mezereum* is however deservedly the most popular and one that, in the words of the catalogue, 'should be in every garden.' Blooming in winter with bare twigs tightly enwreathed with four pointed stars of rich mauve pink it has few rivals to spoil its almost solo effort. The scent is one of the most lovely of all flower perfumes.

Plants can be grown on a short trunk perhaps a foot high but I prefer the plant when it forms a thicket of branches close to the ground. If the top is pinched out of a young seedling plant it will break out to make the wider form.

The flowers are followed by shining scarlet berries that are poisonous. The shrubs are propagated by seed and the young seedlings grown in pots so that they may be moved to their permanent quarters with as little root disturbance as possible. They do not like being moved, are upset by any digging or deep cultivation nearby, and dislike raw farmyard or heavy manuring.

There is a good white form, and some inferior ones, and these all have golden berries.

Forsythia

The name of this popular family commemorates William Forsyth, one of the small band of men who helped to found the Horti-

126

cultural Society, later to become the R.H.S. If he had chosen himself, he could have hardly found a better memorial. Indeed the genus shows qualities that he must have owned himself, for by all accounts he was a vigorous tough character. He was assistant to Phillip Miller who was in charge of the Apothecary's Garden at Chelsea. Forsyth manoeuvred himself into the chief position when Miller was over eighty. He became gardener to the king and did very well by a grant from the public purse for a plaster that he alleged would rejuvenate old and failing trees. Though, of course, it was soon proven useless, it was widely acclaimed for a while. Horticulture seems to attract rather more than its share of spectacular specious claims and downright frauds.

intermedia spectabilis F. suspensa x *F. viridissima*.

This has for long been the most popular of the genus. Now a number of newer hybrids are entering into competition. *Spectabilis* is a strong grower crowding its stems with large deep yellow flowers.

suspensa March April China

There are several forms of this species. The most lax being called *sieboldii* and best trained on a wall or left to scramble over a slope. The most sturdy has been called *fortunei* and this can be grouped successfully in the open. This one will form a mound perhaps 10 feet high of arching, falling, entwining narrow branches. Against a wall any form will provide a curtain of falling stems. It can go up to almost any height against a wall. The clusters of golden flowers are carried on last year's wood in the early spring.

127

From the American Arnold Arboretum have arrived a number of valuable hybrids. By crossing *intermedia* with *japonica* came a number of plants of which two are in commerce in this country. 'Arnold Dwarf' grows only two or three feet high but will go three times as wide. It has smallish limey yellow flowers. 'Arnold Giant' is of the more orthodox upright habit and has large hanging golden bells. Probably the two hybrids that are going to prove most useful are 'Lynwood' and 'Beatrix Farrand.' 'Lynwood' is a very happy character dressing itself with garlands large rich yellow flowers. The flowers are quite distinct from others by being very much wider in the petals and consequently that much more effective. 'Beatrix Farrand', from a colchine induced tetraploid and the very early flowering *F. ovata,* is upright, robust and very thick in growth. The blossom is a rich glowing gold, the individual flowers being easily an inch across.

Garrya elliptica. 12 feet winter W. America.

This evergreen is one usually seen against a wall, or near a wall, and in some parts of Britain it will need the warmth of a wall to survive and flourish. In other parts it will make a thickly clothed dark green bush that is at its most interesting and attractive in the winter months. Then it hangs itself with many grey, green and silver catkins, the male shrubs far outshining the females in length and splendour. Male catkins may be up to a foot long.

It is best where it is a little sheltered from cutting winds, and where it is kept warm and perhaps a little on the dry side. In such a position a small plant will soon get into fast strong thick growth.

Genista

This is a large family, many tender, some rather straggily, and some most excellent garden shrubs. At different times we have grown a lot of these but I think my favourites are *G. cinerea*, *G. hispanica*, and *G. pilosa*. Like Cytissus these are best planted out as small young plants.

cinerea 10 feet June July S. W. Europe

A very showy rather late blooming species with many clustered golden flowers on its long reaching quivers of branches.

hispanica 6 inches May June S. W. Europe

A genista with more than a little of the hedgehog or porcupine about it. Seedlings or cuttings soon form a small rounded green hedgehog of sharp spines. The beast continues to grow in a very even way and will go much wider than tall. It will sometimes grow to 30 inches high. It is a most effective plant grown either as a single specimen or a group which will make a broad impenetrable mass. Through May and June the whole lot is smothered below a complete cover of rich glowing gold. It is best brought up the hard way, poor soil and plenty of sun is the recipe. Grown on richer soil the growth is too rapid, and these new softer parts may get killed in the winter and so leave patches of brown in the middle of the gold.

pilosa 1 to 2 feet May June S. Europe and Britain.

This is a most useful broom, quickly growing from small seedlings to form a low thicket of twigs. It will make a thick ground cover on waste ground, on banks, below trees, between shrubs or wherever the shade is not too great to prevent the sun giving the plants a sense of well being.

129

In blossom it is delightful, dressed overall in bright gold.

Hamamelis

All the Witch Hazels are worthy garden plants, producing their maximum floral display through the depth of the winter. *H. mollis* and the hybrids are the best.

mollis

This will often open in time for Christmas and then last in bloom for weeks. The rather sparsely branched angular shrub has large leaves close in appearance to those of the common hazel. The foliage is discarded quite early and the flowers then appear from the buds that stud the firm bare twigs. Each flower is composed of four narrow ribbons of bright yellow each half to an inch long and held by the reddish brown flower centre. Individually the flowers are hardly spectacular, but their cumulative effect is very pleasing especially against a dark background perhaps of yew or holly. They will remain through prolonged frosts.

Hypericum

calycinum 1 to $1\frac{1}{2}$ feet July to September China

The Rose of Sharon is one of the most useful of shrubs able to grow almost anywhere. Certainly it is the first thing that springs to mind for making a thick carpet in half shade below trees. Here it sends a creeping root-cum-branch along the ground, and at intervals dispatches upright stems a foot or so high. These stems carry large solitary flowers, three to four inches of rich gold, very pleasing currency in the months from the end of June till into September. The leaf cover is attractive formed of oval leaves 2 to 3 inches long.

x *'Hidcote.'*

This is a strongly growing shrub soon reaching a few feet high and more through. It bears large crops of big round wide petalled saucers of deep glowing gold.

Jasminium nudiflorum

No winter flowering shrub has had such reams written in its praise and little wonder for it is indestructible as a plant, blooms freely for months·through the winter months, and is easily propagated.

It is not a shrub with a backbone. It can be grown against a wall or with a support, or it may be allowed to scramble naturally over a large rock, a retaining wall or down a bank. It roots where it touches the soil. The many bright yellow solitary flowers open in succession from the beginning of November till March and will stand quite a bit of frost. Whilst it will bloom well in almost any open situation it is most prolific when planted against a warm south facing wall.

It is propagated by layers which form plants in twelve months, or by cuttings a foot long poked six inches in the soil. Inserted in November they will be well rooted and ready for planting out by the end of next autumn.

Magnolia stellata 15 feet March April Japan

Most of the magnolias rule themselves out of our consideration here as they make trees, but *M. stellata* is a low branching shrub. It is too one of the best of the family because it is early into bloom, is long in blossom, and is a reliable and generous bloomer from a very young age onwards. It is a very hardy shrub and, though the early March and April flowers may be spoilt by frost and bad weather, a new batch of flowers soon replaces the injured ones. The flowers are different in form from most magnolias, the petals are a narrow strap shape $1\frac{1}{2}$ to 2 feet long, but the acreage they lack in width they more than make up by their large numbers. With up to a dozen and a half petals to a flower they have far more than is usual in the family. They open snow white, with age they change to pale pink. The widespread form of the flowers with the petal tips reflexing may be easily admired, they are out before any foliage appears. In *M. Stellata rosea* the flowers open pink. A specimen may eventually top 15 feet high but in doing so it will have spread itself about twice this dimension. It branches low and forms a quite dense pattern of strong growth.

Philadelphus Mock Orange Syringa

argyrocalyx 8 feet June July New Mexico

A graceful species of rather spreading form with unserrated leaves, an unusual feature for a *Philadelphus* and one which it shares with the not dissimilar *P. microphyllus*. As *P. argyrocalyx* has larger flowers it will be preferred; in other respects it is at least as good as its relative. Singly or in threes, white flowers 1 to 2 inches across open their swelling buds in a double rank on the outreaching or falling shoots of last summer. This mock-orange's flowers make gentle fun of the common name by smelling rather more of pineapple.

grandiflorus 12 feet July S. E. U.S.A.

Here is a shrub to plant out and forget. In the shrubbery it will

THE ANSWER IS SHRUBS

look after itself, soon outgrowing the planter and producing good dividends of pure white flowers 2 inches across. Not scented.

inodorus 5 feet June S. E. U.S.A.

An unusual species of compact form usually wider than tall and clothed in polished dark green leaves unlike the usual philadelphus dress of pale green. However the dark foliage helps to make a bigger feature of the large square flowers. These are solitary, scentless, and pure white, the four petals overlapping to make a square with the corners knocked off.

lemoinei P. microphyllus x. *P. coronanus*

The name commemorates the French nurseryman who raised this, the first of the improved hybrid philadelphus, and many other fine shrubs including many Lilacs. There are many fine hybrids of rather varied origin grouped together under this name now. For many years 'Virginal' has been one of the leaders. This outdoes some of the others by being double, it beats others in the size of the flowers which may be up to 2 inches across, and it outstrips the performance of many other competitors by arranging more flowers per dense cluster, and more clusters per bush.

pubescens 20 feet June S. E. U.S.A.

A robust animal that, given its head, reaches up level with the rafters spreading itself comfortably, perhaps twenty five feet across or even more. Such growth is admirable if it leads to some worthwhile display, this species certainly pays its rent for it covers itself with glory and many-flowered racemens of pure white, each flower being nearly two inches across. The species has also been called, not unrealistically and rather delightfully, *Philadelphus grandiflorus floribundus,* a noble name for a noble plant.

Ribes

From the gardener's viewpoint the currants split themselves into three sections, the few of beauty, the few of utility, and the many of botanical curiosity.

aureum 8 feet April W. U.S.A.

One of the best of the currants, a spineless one which grows strongly with many stems going up and branching outwards. Pale green foliage. Flowers in 1 to 2 inch racemens are semi-pendant and a bright golden colour, and with a really musky aroma. The individual florets have a long narrow tube behind the petals about $\frac{1}{2}$-inch long. With *R. sanguineum* this is the best of the family.

cereum 5 feet April W. U.S.A.

A neat round bush with rounded foliage grey in leaf. The flowers, long tubed, up to five in a cluster, appear with the new foliage. The flowers are delicately coloured a silky white flushed pink. As the bush blooms very freely it makes a delightful delicate picture in the spring.

niveum 9 feet April W. U.S.A.

This is a gooseberry, armed as such, with leaves rounded and with drooping flowers a couple or four a time and pure white.

roezlii 3 to 6 feet April California

A pretty gooseberry, with thorns, that has more or less downy

134

THE ANSWER IS SHRUBS

gooseberry foliage. Flowers in ones or twos have calyxs of
purple red whilst the small petals are pinky white.

sanguineum 9 feet April W. U.S.A.

The Flowering Currant, so well known, is an excellent shrub
that deserves its popularity. It is one of the most reliable of
flowering plants. It never fails to provide a fine spring display.
'King Edward VII' is one of the best kinds though not as tall
as some. Its flowers are a very rich crimson. *R. s. splendens* has
fine sized flowers of blood red.

speciosum 6 to 10 feet April May California

A most distinguished gooseberry that breaks into very early
leaf. Young shoots are reddish and from their undersides hang
the many rich burgundy red flowers. Individually and by their
hanging habit they echo in miniature the forms of the fuchsia.

Rubus

biflorus 10 feet Himalayas

A raspberry with no beauty of flower and yellow fruit. It grows
strongly from seed. The upright stems are painted with a thick
waxy white, more effective on the stronger growths. Last year's
stems are cut out in the summer to leave the new white stems
ready to make a focal point in autumn and winter.

deliciosus 6 to 10 feet May Rocky Mountains

The best of the family, delicious in blossom not in fruit. It
covers itself with wide open snow white flowers each 2 inches
across, frank and with some of the light grace of butterflies.
It grows well and forms a strong bush with many arching stems
that lend it an air of gracefulness too. The bark peels quite prettily.

135

malifolius 6 feet June W. China

Whilst the last described has foliage like a blackcurrant, this species apes the apple. It is a scrambling shrub with some thorns. The flowers are white, an inch across, and are borne in a wide bunch at the end of the stems in June.

nutans 1 foot June July Himalayas

A running evergreen prostrate species which will irritate the tidy-minded holding labels and with ideas about plants remaining in the stations to which they have been wisely allocated. It is fine on some less disciplined slope where it can root wherever its bristly stems touch the ground. The leaves, in three parts like a clover, bristle below on their veins and leaf-stalks but above they are a healthy glossy green. Flower stems too bristle, but the flowers are all shining white innocence, one and a half inches of it to each bloom.

odoratus 10 feet July to September N. America

A rumbumptious and pleasing shrub. A youngster grows with healthy appetite for good soil and moisture quickly forming a thicket of strong upreaching stems. Leaves of this, the largest leaved of the family, make the vine their pattern and can some-times need the whole of a foot rule to measure their width. The flowers are a rich purple and are clustered at the shoot ends. Individually they may be about 2 inches across, and each looses its store of sweet scent on the midsummer air to emphasise the beauty of one of the best of the genus. With age vigour declines. Older wood is best removed in the winter months when there is supposed to be time enough for such jobs. Pieces may be pulled off and replanted more thinly to start the process again.

A rose pergola provides interesting areas of light and shade

An attractive setting for a pond
Walpole House, Chiswick Mall, W.4   (Mr. & Mrs. J. H. Benson)

"Autumn Joy" in a foliage border

avement plants in a North London garden

n unusual shape container of rough concrete makes an ideal setting for
ck plants

Rose "New Dawn" makes a beautiful setting when grown up the wall of this house in Kensington

thibeticus 6 feet W. China
A rather handsome raspberry with purple stems and much-cut foliage. Flowers are small and purplish.

Syringa Lilacs
I suppose every garden should have a lilac, but if one is to be grown a good one takes just the same space as a poor one. How easily we tolerate the poorer kinds. I would recommend one of the following species or one of the better hybrids such as those mentioned under *S. vulgaris*.
persica 6 feet May From Persia to China
Has been in the country for over 300 years. The lilac coloured flowers are produced in lighter heads than the popular hybrids. The bushes are neat and rounded and the flowers have the characteristic perfume.
reflexa 15 feet June China
This is a strong good shrub with neatly arranged dense cylinders of small white and pink flowers. These rather buddlia-like flower heads may be up to 10 inches long and 4 inches wide, smaller ones being only half these dimensions. The hanging flower heads are scentless.
tomentella 15 feet June W. China
This pleasant lilac has panicles over six inches long and wide. The effect is pale lilac though the individual florets are white inside. The common lilac is over when this one comes into bloom, its scent is similar but not so powerful.
villosa. 18 feet May June N. China
This is a very strong species which is very free with large panicles

of pink lilac blossom. Almost every twig seems to end in these flowers, many panicles nearly or more than a foot long and at least half as wide.

vulgaris 20 feet May E. Europe

The varieties of this are legion, many very close to each other. The double ones are often the more effective. 'President Loubet' is a very dark purple double, 'Souvenir de Louis' 'Spath' is perhaps even darker but a single, 'Miss Ellen Willmott' is a lovely double white.

Viburnum

This is one of those families like Magnolia which do not have poor species, some may be a little less good than the best. Some lean more heavily on their effectiveness in fruit to win points than others. For example,

betulifolium 12 feet China

This deciduous shrub is at its most attractive when carrying wide bunches of round red fruits

x *burkwoodii* 10 feet April May *V. utile* x *V. carlesii*

This is a wide angled evergreen shrub of rounded form with white flowers tightly packed in sweet scented posies two or three inches across. The buds are pink so that the overall effect is pink and white. Its scent is warm and altogether most noseworthy.

carlesii 8 feet April May Korea.

This popular deciduous shrub owes its wide favour to its well packed half spheres of deliciously perfumed flowers, pink in bud becoming white.

fragrans 15 feet November to March China

This was soon recognized for what it was, possibly the best and most reliable winter flowering shrub. It was introduced by Reginald Farrer. It is a robust deciduous shrub growing quickly upright and forming a thicket of such stems and then producing arching growth. It will grow as much through as up. The small posies of flowers will stand a lot of frost. As posies ought, they are perfumed, a pleasing warm soft scent.

The more usual form is one with the green foliage suffused with bronze, with pink flower buds, and with white flowers touched with pink. There is also a green leaved pure white flowered form. Plants raised from seed vary in these characteristics, flower colour, leaf colour, erectness of habit, and height. It is very easy to increase by layering.

x *bodnantense* 16 feet *V. fragrans* x *V. grandiflorus*

V. fragrans has contributed much to the series of fine winter flowering shrubs raised under this name. Whilst the position of *V. fragrans* is quite secure now in our gardens, anyone starting out to plant a garden would probably choose one of the *V. bodnantense* seedlings for a winter flowering representative of this family. 'Dawn' is the best. This is similar in growth to *V. fragrans* and is probably more vigorous still. It has the bronzed foliage. A tiny layered piece rapidly throws up erect stems 10 feet high in two seasons. It carries a good quota of pink and white bunched flowers on a young bush, as it grows larger and thicker the effect of the flower crop multiplies. The flowers and bunches are larger than those of *V. fragrans*.

henryi 12 feet June July China

This is a stiff upright evergreen that looks as if it had aspirations to be a small tree. Firm pyramids of small white flowers are followed by very attractive bunches of fruit that, like some bank balances, change colour. These become red and then finally black.

macrocephilum 10 to 20 feet May China

This large rounded bush may well retain a good quota of its leaves through some winters whilst dropping all in others. The white flattish flower trusses are margined by large sterile ones an inch or more across with the tiny fertile ones gathered in the centre. Often the completely sterile form is grown and in this the many rounded trusses can be six inches across and so form by far the most prolifically flowered of viburnums.

tinus Laurustinus 12 feet November to Spring S. E. Europe

This has been a favourite for well over 300 years and is still one of the most useful of garden shrubs for it forms rich mounds of dark green evergreen foliage and has flowers in the dark months. It is useful for giving some form to the shrubbery and for providing a rich background to brighter things, but it does well itself by producing white or pink flushed flowers whenever encouraged to do so through the winter and into the spring.

tomentosum. 6 to 12 feet June China, Japan

This is a horizontally branching shrub with foliage like a hydrangea and flat umbels of small fertile flowers margined by a few large white ones an inch or more across. The umbels are set in two rows along and above the sidestretching branches and look most delightful, a quiet, refined, and most engaging design. In the variety *plicatum* all the flowers are large and sterile.

140

To make room for the added acreage the 3-inch bunches become more rounded than flat. It is a spectacular shrub in full bloom.

Chapter 8

Roses, Roses, Roses

In Britain, a garden without roses is dangerously close to a contradiction in terms. Even the smallest garden may have its quota, though they may not be stationed in traditional rose garden style. To devote a major proportion of the garden to roses alone, will seem a straightforward plan to the dedicated rosarian who sees the rest of floral creation as so many evolution-ary experiments and dead ends produced on the groping way towards realisation in genus rosa; but most of us will want more variety through the Lord's 12 months than the rose alone can provide. It may be that our roses, banished from the precious open square yards are taken to the walls to bloom by living room and bedroom window. Maybe a scrambling kind is allowed to clamber through a solitary tree decorating its host with a second happening of flower and maybe even fruit. It could be that we limit ourselves to one of the smaller species that can be accommodated in any spot without threatening to dominate its neighbour's space. Of course it may be decided that one of the small plots or borders can be given over to a squad of rose bushes maybe a narrow bed by the house walls perhaps below a window where a bed of one floribunda variety will give colour for months. Underplanted with polyanthus or clumps of daffodils, the border can be bright most seasons. Traditional borders may have at their back a single bush or a group of some strong growing kind like 'Queen Elizabeth' to be treated as shrubs or small trees! In the mixed borders there may be places for hybrid teas and floribundas planted as a single shrub or in small groups. With lower growing plants to the fore and maybe taller ever-greens to the rear, the gracelessness of the naked winter hybrid rose will be mitigated. And this prompts the thought that roses are so much better chosen from living bushes where the habit of the beast may be judged as well as the beauty that can be seen at flower shows or in magnificent colour reproduction in the pages of rose catalogues.

We cannot be without roses. Each will approach the matter of choice differently. For myself; well I can enjoy roses, all roses, not exactly indiscriminately but safe in the knowledge that their performance is not a matter of business concern as it is with our daffodils. An eighth of an inch on a petal, a slight fleck on the trumpet, a twist in the petal, a scarcely discernible difference in colour shade will make a difference between a shilling and a five pound daffodil. A new kind may mean readjusting the values of scores of other daffodils. An older rose has to make way for a new one in the rose grower's catalogue. But in my garden the old may live alongside the new.

A thicket of dog roses is left undisturbed. Species hybrids are treasured. The floribundas and the hybrid teas are pruned and protected. All kinds are enjoyed. I think I probably get the greatest pleasure from the big species hybrids. A bush can grow to a size and form to become a character even without flowers. Maybe they have only a short flowering season but then they are delightful, and out of bloom the bush is more interesting in shape than a hybrid tea. They may have crops of hips to look decorative in the autumn and winter months. I should be sorry not to have even the humble dog rose of the hedgerow with its arching stems holding quantities of orange hips.

Raising rose species from seed can be a hazardous proceeding. It is a very good rose species seedling that knows its own father. Grown in isolation the danger of raising a batch of mongrels is less. We have at different times raised species from seed. Some grow with exceeding great vigour. *Rosa moyesii* is one. If space permits, a thicket can soon be provided by a few seedlings of this kind, a thicket bright with lots of wide dark red single flowers golden-bossed and followed by great orange fruits. Some may appear close to 'Geranium' with its strong red flowers. But the wonderful 'Nevada' leaves its parents at the post. A young plant soon sends out wide reaching branches at all angles from the rootstock. Some are low over the soil, others more upright. Soon an eight foot wide rounded fountain of stretching branches is built up. In June along the branches the buds open to reveal four inch wide single saucer blooms of creamy white. All along each branch are the series of closely held level saucers. The sight is quite breath-taking. The generosity of the bush in providing such quantities of bloom is typical of the family especially many of those close to the species.

A few yards from our oldest bush of 'Nevada' we have one of 'Fruhlingsgold'. This has the same wholesale attitude towards the display of blossom. The bush is only a little smaller, though distinct with its smaller leaves. A short while after 'Nevada'

144

explodes into blossom 'Fruhlingsgold' follows suit, or rather the white follows the gold. Scattered in a fantastic profusion all over the bush the smaller golden flowers in mass provide a focal point for the garden. 'All the gold in Ireland is sticking to the whin.' All our gold was sticking not to the gorse but to 'Fruhlingsgold.' These single flowered roses do have a simple direct appeal that I, for one, find more betwitching, more full of poetry and magic than the doubles.

The doubling of a flower is to my mind usually a disastrous mutation. What is gained in weight and area of petalage is more than lost in grace. Double nasturtiums, double tulips, and double poppies deny their very nature. A case can be made for some doubles like carnations, chrysanthemums, roses and possibly paeonies. Often, the more double the flower and the larger the variety, the more cabbage-looking and disastrous it is. The boss of stamens in the single paeony, chrysanthemum or rose contrasts with the cloth of the petals, the exact complementary ornament.

To double a flower usually means destroying its real character. In a daffodil this is easily seen, the daffodil depends on its unique form for its gracefulness. With the outline of petals and crown or trumpet lost in a proliferation of segments the daffodil is lost, and a new flower or duster is manufactured, an anonymous seeming amalgam of camellia, carnation, rose, brussels sprout or cabbage.

The argument in favour of doubles may point to the added acreage of coloured petalage and to the longer life of the flower. This may well be so, but the reasoning seems burdened with materialistic overtones. The argument is for quantity not for quality. It is not of greater beauty, and certainly not of more magic. Perhaps the double rose has another argument in its favour. The stage at which the majority of us admire a rose most is when its form is still that of a bud. We admire the neat crisp form of youth, not the shapeless billowing disorder of maturity and old age. Most popular breeds of dog never outgrow their childhood, they live in their world of arrested psychological development. They are dependent on humans as a child may be. The double rose when it outgrows its arrested bud-like child-like youth is formless; humans can tidy up the mess of split petals or rain sodden rotting coloured cabbages.

The rose fancier may or may not care for single roses. They may be completely overlooked or can even provoke hostility. But I feel sure the singles or semi-singles are worth a place. I would urge the value of the species. Some of these are suitable for the border, some as isolated specimens in the lawn, some against a wall, some in the wilder parts of the garden. In the border it is always pleasant to find the 'Threepenny Bit Rose' *R. farrerii.* This is a neat dense bush clothed in small leaves, a species that was introduced by Farrer. It blooms with the great legions of roses in June, the pretty coral buds becoming delightful one inch wide glowing pink threepenny bits thoroughly decorating the whole bush. It gives us a second chance to applaud when the leaves approach their end and deck themselves out in shades of orange, red and purple behind the brilliant red fruits.

In the border or shrubbery, where it is in order to have a near rounded mound of rose some 8 to 10 feet high and perhaps 12 to 15 feet through, the yellow flowered R. hugonis will charm. It is not a shrub that needs to be half hidden so that its display of blossom may be enjoyed in its season and then left out of sight and out of mind for the next eleven months. It is not a rose rampant, but a shrub neat and luxuriant. Masses, frothy light masses, of bright green leaves dress the slender often arching stems. But it puts us in its debt for it pays its golden rent promptly, indeed with us it is the first to open, often, whilst the last daffodils are still present and correct. Come the middle of May and the buds that appear all along the pendant branches begin to open and measure their two inches in the bright sun, the only other roses being under glass, a few possibly being hurried into bloom for the N.R.S. Early Competition, the quiet opening to a summer circus of endeavour.

In June comes *R. xanthina spontanea* more properly called 'Canary Bird.' reminding one of lovely *R. hugonis* which it is possibly superior to though hardly as large flowered. It has grown well with us in Northumberland and elsewhere in our travels making a 10 foot bush of leaving arching branches with plenty of leaves made up of many small leaflets. These are hairy below, one of the botanical distinctions from *R. hugonis*. Flowers of shining yellow perhaps an inch and a half across are studded along the branches.

It would be a sorry day if we decided to jettison all the founder species that have helped to build the modern rose. Then we should have to say farewell to *R. damascena*, the 'Damask Rose,' that crossed with *R. indicaflorus* gave the old 'hybrid

147

perpetuals.' We should loose the 'York and Lancaster Rose' *R. d. versicolor* with its round flowers so curiously striped pink and white. A pity it does not grow more strongly and have stronger flower stalks. *R. gallica versicolor, Rosa mundi,* is altogether better blooming, much more free over a longer period with larger loose petalled shining red flowers striped splashed and dotted pink. The 'Damask Rose' is quite a strong one growing rather stiffly to perhaps six or even ten feet high. The bunches often of ten or more flowers perhaps nearly white or any shade to red, are heavily perfumed. The wood is armed with all calibre weapons from heavy large business-like hooked spikes to bristles and token forces of pimples.

We so often lack the room for the grand gesture, the larger plan; we plant a single specimen when we would like a group of half a dozen or more. Whether this is good gardening or not is debatable. In the conflict between building the garden beautiful and growing a wide variety of plants it depends on the individual which pursuit wins. Most of us blend the plants-man with the creative gardener; some will find more pleasure in studying and satisfying the requirements of each individual plant and getting to know them, whilst others find their greatest pleasure in the completed canvas, the garden picture as a whole. The plantsman will make his professional hole, spread out the roots of a single *R. spinossissima altaica* and plant it firmly. The creative gardener will mass a number as a group. In the flowering effect the c.g. wins, for each extra shrub in the group does not only add its quota of blossom and beauty but multiplies by some mystic factor the beauty of the whole. A solitary rose is beautiful a group of five is far more than five times as splendid.

The 'Scotch Rose' or 'Burnet Rose,' *R. spinossissima* is a variable creeping dwarf bush crowded with small leaves. *R. s. altaica* is quite distinct. For a start it grows twice as high, perhaps six or more feet. The flowers are larger at three inches, being perhaps double the size of the type. A mound of *altaica* covered in creamy white roses can be a sight of magic and splendour at the end of May or the beginning of June.

The lovely *R. macrantha* is a child of nature. Its name, sounding all specific respectability, means simply having long flowers. It is one of a large bunch of wild hybrids probably from *R. gallica,* one of the founders of todays hybrid roses crossed with a form of the 'Dog Rose.' It is probably the best of this bunch. It rears itself erectly up to six or seven feet and smothers its all with clusters of large single flowers. The buds, may be five in a bunch, are pink and the flowers as they expand to their individual span of three or four inches are blushing, but then they become pure white. It grows hardily and well.

We have just planted again the yellow 'Banksian Rose,' *R. banksiae lutea,* which we used to have in Essex. There against a wall and with more sun than most of the British Isles is blessed with, we were happy to get the rose climbing and to enjoy its single yellow flowers, individually small but many in each cluster. We have south facing walls here that may well encourage it to do as well, though it is more than a little doubtful if we shall ever emulate the French 30 to 40 foot specimens.

Not every small garden is going to have room to have a wild garden or a wilder corner, though it could be done. In

149

our wild garden we are inviting back old friends. We have hollies and other dark leaved shrubs for *R. moschata* to scramble over. Here we shall watch the tremendous lengths of young growths being thrown up over any support they can find. We look forward to seeing the primrose and white flowers borne in tremendous bunches, great fifteen inch wide bouquets of many $1\frac{1}{2}$-inch single roses. They are pale yellow in bud and youth but become white. We have planted *R. candata* to build up vigorously its framework of strong branches to perhaps well over twelve feet high and wide. The bright red roses, that in small bunches generous ornament the woodwork, will again please us with their wide eyed appeal, their two inches of colour and their abundance. We already have the 'Dog Roses' to give us fleeting pink blossom and very persistent hips through the autumn and winter. We would all be reading special articles on the beauty of *R. canina's* fruit if only it were a newly dis-covered plant from China or some far off spot. Familiarity may blind us to one of the best of berrying shrubs. I have yet to add *R. davidii* which we shall do for its fruits. It has the vigour that plants need that come under my care, or rather lack of care. It will soon make its presence seen and maybe felt with its plentiful supply of spines over its wide spreading rather loose form. Perhaps it will reach ten feet high or more or may be only half this height. Whatever its dimensions its branches will be sure to carry heavy loads of bright pink two inch flowers to be followed in the bleaker months by the many drooping bunches of large rich red hips. I tend to plant up shrubs that are of interest in the autumn and winter as then the minutes are not quite so precious and crowded as through the daffodil, blooming, lighting, dispatching and replanting times.

Even though the fine *R. wichuraiana* rambler hybrids must claim places in the garden we shall try to find some sunny bank for the mother and father of them. From dear old 'Dorothy Perkins' onwards we have reason to be thankful to *R. wichuraiana* but these ramblers are all more upright plants. The species throws out shoots up to ten or even fifteen feet long in one growing season but keeps them low, scarcely a foot high. The vigour of the shrub on a sunny bank is something splendid to enjoy. The branches are all muscle but the thick clothing of foliage is just as pleasing, with larger leaves than many kinds rich in colour and highly polished. It is late coming into bloom, with bunches of perhaps six to a dozen roses held above a carpet of leaves in July and August. Each is two inches of pure white innocence. There they stand shining, chaste, and with a hint of cold aloofness, like so many debutantes—of the old fashioned kind.

From a rose, 'Max Graf', of a very similar habit to *R. wichuraiana* but with much larger single pink flowers, the famous German breeder Wilhelm Kordes managed to get four seedlings. One of these has been the founder of a new family of repeat flowering climbers. 'Hamburger Phoenix' was one of the first to be acclaimed. This is a stronger grower with handsome large dark foliage and large clusters of red flowers like a floribunda. The crimson colouring makes it the obvious replacement for the old favourite 'Pauls Scarlet Climber.' But perhaps a better one is the later introduced 'Parkdirektor Riggers' which does

151

keep on producing masses of very rich scarlet red flower
through autumn until winter has set in. The flowers are single
or only semi-double and measure about a couple of inche
across, which is not large individually but they are conjure
up in great profusion. 'Leverkusen' varies the pattern by being
a nice rather pale yellow with a heavy initial crop of bloom and
smaller quantities following. In the yellow range of climber
we might choose 'Royal Gold' as one of the best deep yellows
The flowers would do credit to a H.T. 'Golden Showers' i
aptly named, a plant with good glossy deep coloured leave
and a continual succession of bright flowers from the beginning
of summer until nearly wintertime.

As a family we are hopelessly divided over roses. I favou
the species, the climbers and the ramblers and miscellaneou
oddments. The floribundas I enjoy vastly, the H.T.s I admire
I prefer the shape of the floribunda bush, the quantity of flowe
and their long flowering period. I plant 10 floribundas to on
H.T. I suspect a real rose man puts H.T.s first, second and third
The difference is between the viewpoint of the florist fancie
who may be an exhibitor and the gardener. Father plant
nothing but H.T.s. Jean likes to cut the flowers and is happ
with anything which can be cut. She finds the bushes, out c
bloom, awkward untidy and graceless.

The choosing of roses is a difficult business, there are s
many good ones. I find the yellows, pinks and reds mor
pleasing than the whites, the bicolors, and the mixed flam
colours. We do not completely forbid them space, 'Iceberg
is acknowledged as a good free flowering clear white. W

ulus Humulus Aurea

Another example of a pergola, this time in a Kent garden

have had a dozen 'Alison Wheatcroft', the sport from 'Circus', but its rich orange chrome flowers flushed and edged crimson though semi-double and fragrant nevers impresses me as much as well grown all yellows like 'Allgold' or one of the newer yellows. 'Allgold' is a good thing still, free flowering, its colour unfading and the scent of its 2 inch semi-doubles quite discernible. 'Goldilocks' is hardly as tall, but it does have large quantities of small double flowers in shades of gold and yellow that fade to cream. 'Yellowhammer' with semi-double flowers rather larger than 'Allgold' is a good rich gold that does not fade. But these yellows are of the old school of floribundas. The Great British Public seems to want floribundas with H.T. flowers. Now we grow 'Geisha Girl' with beautiful large bunches of fully double golden flowers. We also have the very richly coloured magnificent 'Chinatown', a terrifically robust bush with glowing deep large flowers that might have been grafted on from a H.T.

Yellow and golden shades are the colours that I feel shine out most effectively in the garden. Certainly from a distance this is so. But where one is constantly walking the richer reds are very satisfying. But even here I find the orange scarlet more happy than the deep crimson shades. We grew a bed of 'Moulin Rouge' for a while and they gave a very good quota of velvety crimson semi-double flowers, but it would not compare for immediate impact with 'Sarabande', 'Highlight' or the bright 'Orangeade'. 'Sarabande' has 'Moulin Rouge' as one parent. Like its parent it does have a long season, being very effective in the autumn but in this late season 'Highlight' can

153

TYPES OF ROSES

HYBRID PERPETUAL

HYBRID TEA

MOSS ROSE

FLORIBUNDA

RAMBLER

SINGLE

perhaps just outdistance even 'Sarabande.' 'Sarabande' has really dazzling scarlet semi-double flowers in very generous trusses. The flowers are over three inches across and are produced for month upon month. 'Highlight, is just that shade lighter, a fuller but smaller flower but carried in good trusses. The plant has all 'Sarabande's' vigour, perhaps being even a shade more upright still. 'Orangeade' has a luminous quality that must be bound up with the texture of the flowers as well as with the rich scarlet pigment. The colour around the boss of stamens is dazzling, one of the best in its class. Its strong growth gives good crops of flowers carried in many small trusses or independently; in the trusses the flowers are well arranged, none are lost below or are crowded out of contributing their percentage to the total effect.

A degree less deep in colour shading are flowers like 'Anna Wheatcroft, a single flowered variety of abundant strength and good healthy habits. Being more or less single the flowers are rather larger at three to four inches than more doubled kinds, as one would expect. The charm of the single flower is here well represented, the rich velvet texture can be admired the whole width of the bright scarlet petals whilst the boss of pale apricot stamens fully complements the richer colouring. 'Dickson's Flame' has perhaps one quality in common, the purity of its colour pigment. But this strong kind has rich scarlet blossom, but more doubled and with a more generous allocation of perfume. It has the vigour of a pop singer in full cry, fortunately it looks, behaves and smells more like a good rose.

One of the more interesting floribundas that we have

recently planted is 'Rose of Tralee,' though it is perhaps not right to think of this as a floribunda as it makes a distinct bush. It has the free flowering orange scarlet 'Korona' as father and the pale golden Kordesii climber 'Leverkusen' as mother. It is proving a strong bushy plant quick to get into strong growth and giving good crops of large double roses through the summer and into autumn. The colour is a rich warm pink, the petals becoming pale gold at the base and with a touch of this colouring on the reverse.

'Queen Elizabeth' has become a popular hedging variety with its strong upright growth. Certainly it is most effective so used, especially if lower growing bushier types are planted in front to avoid any suggestion of bareness lower down the tall reaching stems. Its rich green foliage and many double clear pink flowers borne in small bunches or singly make a beautiful as well as an effective hedge.

Amongst the pinks I would be sorry to be without 'Ma Perkins' with the familiar quite large double rather tight formed roses in their many small sweet scented bouquets. Its shades of deep and paler pinks are very pleasing. But even more a favourite is 'Dainty Maid' with its large trusses of single flowers of creamy yellow pink and richer pink. Its strong habit and free blooming disposition make it an 'old favourite.' But these old stagers have to make way in the catalogues for newer things.

As a nurseryman I cannot afford to be guilty of any suggestion of heresy. The New must be better than the Old. Certainly there are plenty of post-'Dainty Maid' pinks of great charm and beauty. 'Dearest' must rank as one of the best. It has really

156

full bodied fragrance to add to the attraction of the many nicely spaced trusses of doubled round blooms of shining rose pink with an underlying suggestion of salmon. Against polished foliage through the summer the scent and the colour of 'Dearest' does enchant. 'Elizabeth of Glamis' in a rather different role cannot be overlooked. It comes from 'Spartan' x 'Highlight.' It has many qualities to help it maintain a treasured space in gardens for many years. Beautiful in bud, of good H.T. form, it is a large flower of engaging colour, a blend of warm pink and salmon, and bewitching fragrance. It opens out nicely to show more of its pink colouring, the salmon gold suffuses the reverses and the bases of the petals. The trusses are not over-crowded and are produced in long succession above the healthy foliage. With flowers like this the older conception of the floribunda changes. The rosarian who believes real roses to be H.T.s may hesitate as he counts the petals of the 'Peace' or 'Montezuma' and looks at 'Elizabeth of Glamis.'

The H.T.s

The hybrid teas are meant to be looked at individually, their blooms seen, touched, smelt and admired. I take the difference between floribundas and hybrid teas to be in the same order as dinner wines and old brandies. But the high noon of summer that sees the H.T.s at their best sees me breathing heavily, eating quickly, and dashing frantically to ensure that last month's work is completed this month before the avalanche of next month's overcomes us. At least that is how it often feels.

Time to stand and stare is at a decidedly heavy premium. Flori-bundas we have for effect. But some H.T.s must be grown, trying to avoid the ones that look so dismal in wet weather and the ones that grow with such headstrong vitality that a helicopter is nearly a necessity to enjoy the flowers.

Yellow is the colour of the sun, of youth, of strength. As a substitute for all three I always enjoy the yellows most. I still enjoy 'Spek's Yellow' with its tall flowering stems carrying neat rich yellow blooms. One has to include 'Peace' for its terrific strength, healthy polished foliage and great blooms of pale gold edged pink. The body colour varies from deep yellow to creamy light yellow but it is always pleasing. One has to remember that one is planting a small tree rather than a small rose when planting 'Peace' and its kinsfolk, and of course it does best when not pruned too hard. Combining some of the qualities of both these last two as its parents is 'Gold Crown.' It has very large full flowers with some of the long pointed 'Speks Yellow' bud form. Its deep gold makes it one of the foremost yellow bedding roses, though it will have to fight with 'Kings Ransom' for first place. This last is a really well shaped, rather chastely formed, rich yellow that is a very free reliable bloomer and a decent sized bush. 'Perfecta', that everyone raves about, is certainly not my rose of this or any other year. It is too big to own and keep the shape that should complement the colour; the cream overlaid, suffused, and veined in rich pink I find less than bewitching. 'Grandmere Jenny' in the 'Peace' idiom is creamy gold edged with rich pink but for my money I prefer the richer shades of a kind like 'Beaute.' It is a nice long pointed form in a full, but not overfull, flower of gold and rich apricot that I like. It has the rich green foliage and strength of the 'Peace' type. 'Sutters Gold' borders on orange, for its body colour would be called a pale orange by most and this rich colouring is suffused or overlaid in red.

But 'Sutters Gold' is about as far as I would go in splattered impressionistic mixed colour essays. Mixed flame colours in 'Bettina' I can admire, but it is not very restful and I go to someone else's garden to admire its healthy growth and good perfume. The bicolors too seem to lack the serenity that I look for in a perfect rose. 'Piccadilly' tempts one of my mind to break the rule and include it in their collection. It is rich strong scarlet inside and golden yellow outside. As the buds begin to open more, the red begins to shine through the gold. Its colour is well retained making it perhaps the best of the bicolors. 'Wisbech Gold' is a 'Piccadilly' seedling with a generous disposition in dealing out huge golden blossoms. The bright red edge will attract some but seems to me a somewhat un- neccessary gilding of the rose. To turn to the reds is to be confronted by an embarrassment of riches. The rose is meant to be red. All like the red rose, some love the red, red rose, whilst others find the red, red, red rose, the deepest possible shade the best. For myself I confess I find the dark black red roses of 'Madame Louise Laperriere' and similar kinds a heady kind of beauty. One could dive into the sea of perfume and be pleased to drown. But one dark, dark, red rose will suffice. The scarlets and orange reds are happier colours. Some find 'Super Star' a difficult colour to live with or for other roses to live by. I acknowledge something of the 20th century neon light glare in 'Superstars' vermilion salmon red, but for better or worse we live in the 20th century and provided this iridescent rose is kept clear of other orange reds it can be admired for its neat form or scent as well as the rich colour. 'Wendy Cussons' in more traditional red shades of cherry scarlet is a must for its fine shape and rich fragrance. And of course 'Ena Harness' is another essential variety, a rich crimson scarlet of excellent chaste form and full blooded perfume. Also in deep tones of crimson and scarlet the 'Josephine Bruce' will always be amongst my favourites. It makes a good bush with dark foliage and an abundance of bloom. Taller growing is 'Karl Herbat', a prodigy of vigour with 'Peace' as a mother. Beautifully formed deep red large flowers are a little paler on the reverses. We have other reds about us but these tried ones are still the favourites. 'Montezuma' with its terrific foliage and huge flowers of glowing salmon has become a new favourite. 'Uncle Walter' grows with great strength and is giving dark red large sized blooms. 'Papa Meilland' with fragrance and rich dark red seems to crown a tradition, a flower of dark blood evoking a sense of stillness and timelessness.

A pink rose to have me reaching for an order form must be a full rich pink, the 'Perfectas' are not for me. I am happy with 'June Park' with its large pink flowers and rich scent. 'Eden Rose' with its deep madder pink petals with their silvered reverses please me, though I fancy 'Isabel Ortiz' has the edge on 'Eden Rose.' The paler pinks leave me cold but some richer kinds that mix their pink with orange may be acceptable. 'Shot Silk' in a mixture of shades is jolly. 'Show Girl' is welcome for its deep pink and long pointed buds.

Blue, lilac, lavender, grey, wishy washy, or whatever you like to call them; these I find interesting and at times most beautiful. The form of 'Sterling Silver' with long pointed flowers is enjoyable, but we have replaced this by 'Intermezzo' which is a stronger plant with deeper coloured flowers. It is by no means the last word but it is at least a stronger garden plant than Sterling Silver' and the flowers are a shade deeper. 'Lilac Time' too finds a place with its tall reaching stems and its many long pointed deep lilac buds. It has a nice scent.

And for whites I cannot find my pulse racing at any dangerous speed when contemplating any of the traditional hybrid teas. But alone as a specimen shrub I am happy to have the 1900 'Frau Karl Druschki' with its very large well formed snow white flowers produced freely over a large strong bush.

But of the varieties of rose there is no end.

Chapter 9

Border Trouble

Jean and I earn a mild living as nurserymen, ninety-nine pennies out of a hundred coming from the daffodils we grow and sell as bulbs. We work many hours a day and with three children around us sometimes wonder at 'The Problem of Leisure.' We pay cash for the groceries we collect each weekend and when back home I sometimes get gently bullied into doing something about the borders.

The truth is that the border is a compromise beast and a time absorbing one. In our technological age we are constantly being badgered into thinking in terms of increased productivity and efficiency. The border is technologically an inefficient unit. How can one site provide ideal conditions for the variety of plants growing in it. In the best British tradition we make the best we can of the compromise.

The technological philosophers tell us that our purpose in life is 'to promote the maximum fulfilment of the evolutionary process.' We live in the psychological evolutionary phase. It must be a comfort to the commuters that daily pack themselves into trains and tubes to think of themselves as the psychological evolutionary spearhead. Little wonder that, with the multifarious and ever increasing pressure of modern existence that gardening is such a widespread leisure time occupation. It is a safety valve for the release of the built up repressions and pressures of week-day work. We take it out on the groundsel and the bindweed and return refreshed to the psychological evolution.

The herbaceous border, the undiluted herbaceous border of before 1914, is an almost extinct animal. It takes too much training. It lives on in folk's memory, in one or two stately homes, and on the tops of chocolate boxes. Nowadays the border may contain the traditional herbaceous plants but shrubs have advanced and help to give the border permanent architectural form, bulbs aid the early spring display before the herbaceous plants get into their full stride, alpines find a foothold in the front and occasionally even a small tree like an almond or a cherry may burst into a pink cloud above all else. The border then is a diversified production unit, a mongrel in design. It is a canvas allowing the tachist painter to splatter geraniums, nemetia, salvia, and ageratum etc. in random kaleidoscopic effect, the expressionist may rear up the bold rhubarb, *Rheus palmatum rubrum*, against the hedgehog *Veronica cuppressoides;* the surrealist may surround Bleeding Hearts with Lamb's Tails, a neo-PreRaphaelite may allow ivy and periwinkle to trail behind a moss rose and a group of auriculas; again the Pop Art enthusiasts may use gnomes, broken wheelbarrows, lamp-posts and posters of 'Miss Weedkiller 19—?' around a few Gooetia and marigolds.

But so much for the armchair, now outdoors and into the border. The dimensions of the border are similar to those of a piece of string, but as a general rule the wider the border the more effective it is. A long border will allow almost any width,

163

even a medium length border will allow a width of eight to ten feet. To make the most of this width it is a wise move to arrange for the back to be higher than the front, a difference of six, nine, or twelve inches will add this much to the stature of the rear plants. The stage is sloped, the auditorium of path or lawn is level for our convenience.

Sometimes if the border is not of uniform width but becomes wider as it goes away from the house, this heightening the back of the border may be quite dramatic. It may be thought worthwhile if the border is a wide one to build up with bricks or rocks the back half so that there are in fact two terraces in the border and even the terraces can be sloped.

The first plants to be stationed in the border will be the evergreen shrubs, assuming for the moment that we are not planting anything quite as large as a standard cherry. One of the dark leaved *Berberis* species of hybrids might be used, perhaps a group of three *B. darwinii* might serve in the background and soon form a dark mass with miniature holly foliage and their beautiful gold and orange blossom. We might use the upright columns of some junipers or even the fastigate yew, *Taxus baccata fastigiata*. Maybe we can use one of the virburnums. Lower down we could certainly make use of the hedgehog form of the double flowered gorse, a tidy pleasing rounded mass of grey green spines that covers itself with long lasting masses of rich gold.

Then, we might turn to planting a few of the deciduous shrubs that we certainly need. A really wide border may give enough room for the vigour of the forsythias. Here where room is at a

164

premium we can abandon our rule of three and plant only one plant of F. 'Lynwood,' for each plant has the strength of three and produces a mass of strong branches that reach up and arch over so that in the spring when the bare branches are suddenly festooned with golden blossom it would seem the earth is gushing a fountain of gold. Some room must be allowed for this vigorous spendthrift, but the smaller slower growing *Daphne mezereum* will not need so much space and can be planted close to the front of the border. Here is a plant that is best planted in three or even dozens if there is the space, for it blooms generously and without fail in the winter months. As we have planted them close to the edge of the border we can the more easily enjoy its rich perfume. Sometimes these shrubs can be leggy. This effect is less noticeable where three are going into each other, but, if one can harden ones heart, surgery at an early age can also help to provide the shape of bush we want. If we cut back the main stem and encourage the lower ones to branch outwards we shall soon have a wide dense bush that will be the glory of the border each winter.

Again towards the back of the border we may find we have room for a plant or more of the Witch Hazel. *Hamamelis mollis,* which is the best species and the earliest to bloom. We usually rely on our largest one to provide golden ribbons for Christmas. It is a sparsely branched shrub and no rampant grower so that it will not usurp too much of its neighbour's soil or airspace. If the border is not swept by holocausts from Siberia we might plant a bush of *Garrya elliptica* in the open. Here we have returned to an evergreen but a most unusual one. It forms a dense bush

BORDER PLANTS

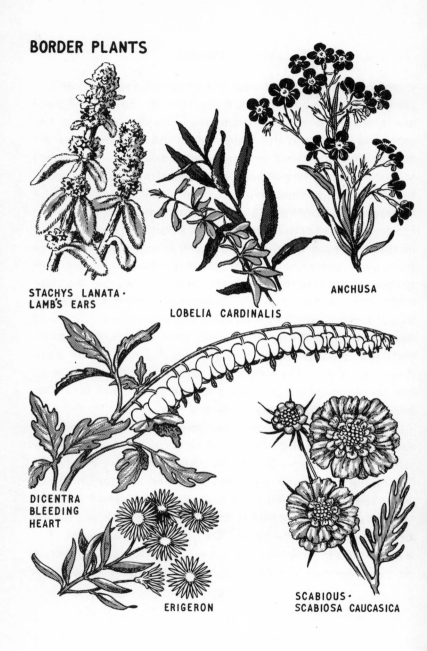

STACHYS LANATA·
LAMB'S EARS

LOBELIA CARDINALIS

ANCHUSA

DICENTRA
BLEEDING
HEART

ERIGERON

SCABIOUS·
SCABIOSA CAUCASICA

of dark green leaves and produces masses of very long winter catkins in a fascinating design of grey green and pale yellow. In the North it is more usual to grow this fine shrub against a wall to give it just that extra bit of protection that it enjoys in a cooler climate.

To the forefront of the border it would be a shame not to enjoy a few heathers. Some of the *E. carnea* varieties would make dense low masses of foliage and provide winter blossom. A few sprigs of flower from one of these easy low growing plants can help to make very pleasing little table decorations or be incorporated in some other indoor flower arrangement.

Then we might well turn our attention away from the shrubs proper and think of the other border characters. We could start thinking about our foliage effect and plant groups of *Hostas,* perhaps the golden variegated *aureomarginata* or the blue green *gigantea* sometimes called *H. glauca robusta.* By these we could by contrast plant some of the swordlike foliage of the irises. Or remembering the leaves beloved by countless generations of sculptors and carvers we could add some of the indestructible roots of *Acanthus.* We may try the heart shaped leaves of *A. mollis* with its stiff spikes of lilac pink flowers standing perhaps three feet high, or maybe the deeply cut long leaved *A. spinosus* with spiny protection and even taller spikes densely packed with purplish flowers. Again we could turn to the long lived ever interesting hardy ferns in their very many kinds. True that some of the kinds treasured by our great grand-parents have been lost, but there is a revival of interest in ferns and there are still a good number to choose from.

167

If some enterprising person or concern were to start producing ferns on a large scale I feel sure that he would be backing a winner especially if new types were bred. Research workers have found it extraordinarily easy to produce mutants of ferns and many of these are both interesting and attractive.

But the number of plants that can be employed in the border is legion. It is not really part of this book to try to enumerate them. But as we are concerned with effect and their use we can pause to consider a few. I shall mention a mere handful that I enjoy, some common some less often seen.

Polyanthus

Does it seem strange to spend time over such a familiar plant? I give it room for two reasons. The modern polyanthus is a fine border plant and can provide masses of attractive colour over quite a large number of weeks. The second reason is that we can use this plant as an example of the value of picking the very finest strain that one can. A poor flowered plant takes as much looking after as a good one and as seed is the least of our expenses it pays to buy the very best.

Perhaps memory plays me false by glamorising the past, but the first border I remember seemed to have every spare inch stuffed with multicoloured polyanthus. What strain these were goodness knows. Now I would restrict myself to possibly three strains, though there are other good ones on the market. I am an admirer of the work of the great plant breeder Frank Reinelt and enjoy his 'Pacific Strain' of Polyanthus as well as his magnificent delphiniums and begonias. Noone in Britain can ignore Blackmore and Langdon's strains of polyanthus. The difference between these two strains is not so great now I believe as it once was. The Pacifics can be larger and the colour range is perhaps wider with some of the colours being a little richer, on the other hand Blackmore and Langdon's strain of plants do seem to be rather longer lived. Both are very fine and a real testimonial to the work of the breeders. Coming to the fore now are the Barnhaven primroses now at home in the Lake District. In this strain we have a very free flowering plant with large flowers in many different bright colours and shades. All three strains have been worked upon for many years and careful work is done to maintain and improve the strains each flowering season.

The 'Pacific Strain' is the result of work going back to 1928. To start with Mr. Frank Reinelt collected all the most promising plants that he could find to grow together in Capitoll, California. He bred with these and in 1934 culled his stock to 50 which became the foundation of the modern strains. 5,000 plants were raised in the first year. Each season only the finest few plants were selected as parents for the next generation. The result of this selection was a very remarkable improvement in vigour, flower size, forms and colours. The number of plants raised annually increased slowly to 200,000. Three million plants were tested in 30 years.

In the spring Mr. Reinelt chooses the best plants to raise from the fields to have potted up for the cross pollination necessary to produce the high quality seed he sells. These plants represent less than 1% of those in the fields.

Stems can often be a foot high and are very stout. Wide well arranged heads come in colours from brilliant reds, through a variety of reddish pinks, pinks, salmons, apricots, oranges, golds, yellows, rusts, deep navy blue, mid-blue, and powder shades to violets as well as whites. Every shade is represented. All are terrifically strong, often blooming in the autumn as well as the spring. After a couple of seasons they tend to lose some of their initial strength. They do make fine pot plants and can be made to bloom from the beginning of the year.

Seed is best sown early in the year, say February. There should be a 90% germination within two or three weeks. A seed compost of 1 coarse sand, 1 loam and 2 coarse peat is what we use. The soil has to be kept moist all the while, pots or boxes can be enclosed in polythene. When the seedlings have two true leaves they are ready for transplanting into seedboxes or cheap whalehide or polythene pots. In a further 12-14 weeks the plants are fully strong enough for planting in their permanent places. By the autumn many will have flowers. They grow best in positions where they have some protection from the strongest summer sun.

The native primrose is such a charming plant it seems almost indecent to start mixing new colours to paint the pale flowers that peep out of the soft green mound of foliage from New Year till the last of the daffodils fade away. Nevertheless the hybrid primroses are most attractive and are perhaps more amenable to the rough and tumble of the garden borders than the primroses of the hedgerows. They are easy plants to grow and are very persistent. Most colours found in Polyanthus are also found in primroses but often in a softer hue. The blue primroses are established favourites and range from pale powder blue to navy. Some of the dark ones with lemon eyes are very striking.

The primroses differ from polyanthus in their germinating habits. Whilst seed of polyanthus sown early in the year will germinate very evenly, a proportion of the primrose seed sown at the same time does grow but the remainder germinates at intervals later, probably a defence mechanism that ensures that if one set of seedlings does not meet with favourable conditions to continue the species another will.

Primulas

The primula genus offers many candidates for the border. We used to grow colonies of the drumstick primrose, *P. denticulata,* in shades from the pure white to deep purple and burgundy. Grouped together it is most attractive and it can certainly be a long lived plant, growing quickly from seedlings to give many round heads of crowded flowers in the drumstick form. They will seed themselves freely if the soil is left undisturbed and will exist for decades below light trees, between shrubs, on banks, or by hedgerows.

Some of the rarer primulas, though interesting and beautiful, hardly rank as borderworthy characters. The most successful are the more generally grown species. In damper, shady spots some of the candelabra types are easy and effective. The work that the late Hew Dalrymple did with these primulas is a testimony to his patience and plantsman's genius. At his home and lovely garden at 'House in the Wood,' Bartley, this retiring and

most modest of men quietly and carefully built up a fine collection of many kinds of plants. Today we remember him
chiefly for his *Primula pulverulenta* 'Bartley Strain.' The typical
P. pulverulenta is taken to be a deep red flower with a darker
eye. From these wild forms have been raised various reds, and
the most lovely rose and pink forms. Stems can reach three feet
high and have five or more whorls of outward facing flowers,
each an inch to two inches across. The damper the site the
most robustly they grow. Planted as seedlings in a colony their
strong growth soon produces a ground cover that does not
allow weeds to sow themselves.

Auriculas have had a long history in cultivation. The origin
of the curiously beautiful show kinds has interested many. Sir
Rowland Biffen, in his book 'The Auricula' published after his
death, wrote of his investigations into the origin of the mutation
or mutations that led to the mealy farina of the leaves invading
the flowers, and of the breeding of the precise florist's show
flowers that went on through the second half of the eighteenth
century and from then till the present day. Very high standards
were built up in the heyday of the florist's flowers, the first
half of the last century. Not only were good specimens eagerly
sought after and exhibited at numerous shows but books were
written on their culture and extraordinary care was taken over
the preparation of composts to grow the plants in. One of the
leading growers went to quite fantastic lengths. Sir Rowland
Biffen summarises the advice of I. Emmerton in his 'A Plain
and Practical Treatise on the Culture and Management of the
Auricular,' 1815.

'He was convinced, if not obsessed by the idea, that Auriculas required the richest possible diet, and he set out to provide this by means of a compost as extraordinary as any that has ever been devised. It consisted of three parts of goose dung steeped in bullock's blood, three of sugar-baker's scum, and two of fine yellow loam to which a small quantity of sand might be added if considered advisable. The sugar-baker's scum, he understood consisted of "the dross of sugar a proportion of the West India mould, fine clay, bullock's blood, lime water, etc." The dung and blood were put into a pit covered with a hurdle to keep dogs off. and left to putrefy—much to the annoyance of neighbours. In six weeks or so the pasty mass solidified and was then ready for digging out and mixing with the sugar-baker scum and loam. The mixture was exposed to the sun and air for two years and the heap broken down and raked through and through at monthly intervals. On its richness, mellowness, freedom from insects, weed seeds, and other nauseous properties, Emmerton insists time after time, wearing the reader of his book with continuous repetition.' Biffen points out that, 'Reference to this procedure is much subsequent writing, especially latterly, has been compressed into the statement that, "he used bullock's blood in growing his auriculas," leaving the impression that his cultivation was of a peculiarly macabre nature.'

The show auriculas certainly do not need all this rich feeding, but they often need careful tending to see that they have adequate moisture and are kept free from aphids; certainly they are useless in the border for, even if robust enough to survive, their flowers would be hopelessly smudged by the

BORDER PLANTS

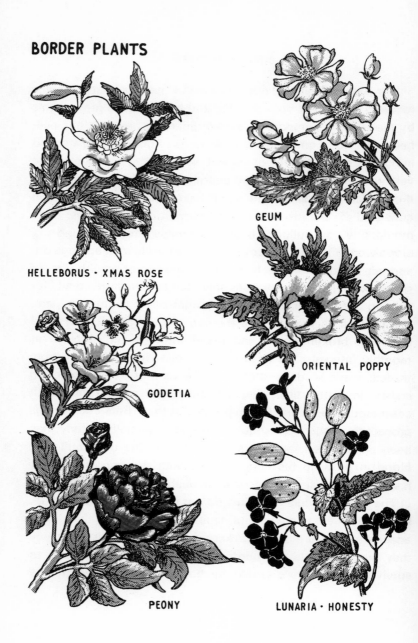

HELLEBORUS · XMAS ROSE

GEUM

GODETIA

ORIENTAL POPPY

PEONY

LUNARIA · HONESTY

slightest bit of rain. The border auricula are a mixed breed of much more hardy plants. Most of these are nameless seedlings. Some have passed from garden to garden. Sometimes they are taken into nursery gardens and are given fancy names. Not infrequently different names have been given to the same plant and more often many different names have grown under one name. One of my favourites is the most attractive pale blue auricula, 'Old Irish Blue,' not dissimilar to some of the somewhat more rounded and precise alpine varieties shown by James Douglas of Great Bookham. 'Old Irish Blue' is a very strong plant very easy to increase from cutting or by division. It is a bright green leaved plant clear of all meal. The flowers are freely produced and are a pale blue that becomes deeper as it reaches the circular pale cream centre. There is an underlying hint of lavender in the blue. It is a delightful border plant and the possessor of a very attractive sweet perfume. There is now on the market another plant offered as 'Old Irish Blue.' It is quite distinct with very dark purple blue flowers. It is a nice flower but I feel sure that it is not the plant previously known as 'Old Irish Blue.'

Hellebores

In 'The Winter Garden' I tried to put the case for the wider cultivation of hellebores, all the other hellebores as well as the Christmas Rose. Not wanting to become somewhat of a bore about hellebores, I shall content myself here with mentioning just one or two that should be included in the border and of again backing the value of hellebores as most hardy plants.

capable of adding interest and beauty to the garden in the very gloomiest months of the year.

Helleborus corsicus is a favourite of mine. Plants are best raised from seed or bought as young seedlings. These always get away to a better start than older specimens. Nothing is lost for young seedlings with single leaves soon start producing their adult divided foliage and become mature plants. The glossy rich green foliage is most handsome and may make mounds a foot or eighteen inches high and wider. The handsome veined foliage is a joy to me at all times, it always looks so strong, luxuriant, and healthy. Towards the end of the year tight flower buds appear between sheaths all pale apple green. One, or in large plants, many pale stems support a branching fountain of pale green blooms. Seedlings vary in their flowers, some having distinctly wider and rounded segments than others. In some the segments flatten out widely, in others they retain their cupped concave form. The pattern of greens, dark and pale, makes a quiet pleasing picture through the winter and into the spring. As the plants grow in size they send up more and more fresh shoots from the rootstock each spring. The old ones die away after they have mothered their crop of seed and after the young reddish shoots have produced fresh lots of the tough shining green foliage.

H. foetidus is in bloom at the same time as *H. corsicus* and has the same tough character whilst also depending on the pattern of green to make its floral appeal. But this plant has its leaves cut more deeply so that it has miniature palm like leaves and these are a very deep green that contrast with the pale green flower stems and the goblet shaped flowers with their pale yellow boss of stamens.

The Lentern Roses, *H. orientalis* hybrids, are fun. They produce taller, more polished and toothed leaves than the Christmas Roses and with 9 to 18 inch flower stalks they are much taller. The flowers are individually smaller but there are many more of them. They vary in colour from white to a purple black. The mauvey pinks are the commonest shades. But the variation does not end simply with the colour, for this may vary in shade in the flowers and these may be unadorned or ornamented with a few or a multitude of darker spots, often crimson, in the centre or spreading over all the flower. Again they may or may not add to their fascination with a distinct heavy plum-like bloom. Some individuals may have rather narrow petals (really sepals) but more often they are wide and overlapping to form wide bowl-shaped blooms. Some make wide flattish stars, others the bowl shapes, and other tighter cup or goblet forms. The variation is virtually endless. Whilst some hybrids have been named and are worthy plants they are not easy to get hold of, not being the easiest of plant to propagate vegetatively and grow commercially. However, mixed colours may be purchased from nurserymen. Perhaps even better results may come from raising plants from some mixed seed. Hellebores are not over-keen on being moved or disturbed so that it may be a positive advantage to grow ones own stock from seed. Inferior individuals can be culled.

Seed sown in autumn in boxes or pots of John Innes seed compost may be left out for a few weeks frosty weather and

then brought under glass. Here the seed should germinate in
the early spring. When the first true leaves are fully developed
the seedlings may be pricked out. This is best done carefully
as the more roots that are broken the longer it will take to make
a flowering plant. The soil should be watered beforehand,
allowed to drain, and then the small plants gently teased out.
If the seed is sown thinly, an inch or so apart, this should be
easy enough. The young plants will be potted up in small clay,
plastic, whalehide or fibre pots using John Innes potting
compost No. 1. They may then be plunged in beds or boxes of
peat or some such material that will help to keep the soil of the
pots moist and at an even temperature. Then a good watering
will set the youngsters on their way. If kept in a cool spot or a
shaded frame, and if the plants are kept moist, they will grow
quite rapidly and be ready for planting out by the end of the
summer. If for some reason they are not strong enough at this
time they may be kept and set out the following spring. In the
border they grow well but they do best in semi-shade perhaps
between shrubs. Here they should not be subjected to root
disturbance. They may begin to open their flowers through the
months of January, February, March and into April. Few flowers
last longer.

Rhubarb, rhubarb, rhubarb
He jumps, you say, from primroses to rhubarb in almost one hop,
just touching down on hellebores between. Where is the rhyme,
the connection between primroses and rhubarb? The answer is

that the border represents an opening meeting, all may come and contribute their piece. A full blown paeony makes a florid point, a delphinium speaks of true-blue principles, the oriental poppy waves red flags, alyssum and aubretia murmur, the periwinkle winks open a bright eye and closes it again. I remember the flowers in our borders past and present as they were growing, all types present, the contrasts between the habits of neighbours making the interest in the border.

Perhaps the word rhubarb lacks a touch of magic and poetry, yet some of the undomesticated species have a noble air about them. I believe the best is *Rheum palmatum rubrum*. It grows tall enough to see eye to eye with its guardian. Perhaps you feel this is too much rhubarb for your border, as it might be in a small one, and if so, it might well be put to do duty in the shrubbery or in some wilder corner. The deeper and richer the soil the more magnificently the broad leaves and tall strong flowering stems grow. Leaves vary in size, but are usually more than a foot long and are all basically a heart shape. The margins are rarely unbroken, being lobed to a varying degree. The upper surfaces of the leaves can be quite rough and in *R. p. rubrum* are flushed with reddish brown. The flowers are a rich deep crimson in a large panicle.

I like rhubarb, but it is not everyone's choice as a cut flower, though it can be most effective in its seeding heads. And of course as I am reminded every now and again we must have flowers to cut. So I have planted some Pyrethrums in one border. We once grew an acre of these for the cut flower market. I can remember cutting and cutting at the things with the flowers

179

SMALL GARDEN DESIGN

head high. They are of course a fine cut flower, they will take a terrific lot of punishment from the time they are cut till the time they are placed in a vase of water. The daisy is a simple frank flower, the pyrethrums as coloured daisies have all the simple direct charm of these. We had to grow 'E. M. Robinson' for its fine clear pink flowers. I expect there are still acres of it. 'Kelways Glorious' we had as an early strong red, and 'J. N. Twerdy' as a double red. Now we are trying the double pink 'Venus' and 'Taurus' as a single red. The 'pyes' are so easy, so prolific, that one tends to overlook their real beauty and the pleasant ferny foliage they retain through the summer months.

To move from pyrethrums to paeonies is to move into the aristocracy of the border. The herbaceous paeony is one of the finest of all garden plants. First it is perennial, one plants a root and it will be there after empires have been made and lost. In youth the young stems reaching from the bare ground are often a most decorative polished burgundy, the young foliage is attractive, the flower buds that seem to promise their display for so long suddenly do burst open and here is silk and satin of the finest to dazzle and delight in pure whites, creams, pinks, reds, some pale yellows and in so many subtle shades it is pointless trying with words to pin them down. We have mentioned varieties in the chapter 'Planning for the Year'.

Some plants one remains faithful to through the years disregarding fashion or difficulty. For me one such plant is *Iris douglasiana*. This is one of a group of wild American irises, a plant that forms a thick tuft of dark green healthy looking leaves over a foot long. Before the main Bearded Irises come

180

into bloom *I. douglasiana* covers its greenery with flowers of lilac and touches of gold. The colours vary a lot, some seedlings are complete albinos, others are a pale grey lavender and all shades are represented to near purple. The intricate veining in darker shades helps to make the flowers more interesting when examined closely. Each flower stem carries a bud in reserve so that after one flower fades another opens. As a child I raised a large series of hybrids from incrossing the various members of this American iris group. They were all nice, many were very delightful. We have never found them plants that enjoy being divided so that I suggest that they are best raised by seed or bought as young seedlings.

For a few pages I have allowed myself the pleasure of recommending a handful of plants, but each gardener will make his own selection. What I would commend now is that it is worthwhile trying to get the best variety, the healthiest stock and that it often pays best to afford the extra few shillings to buy from a reliable source. And a final word; all plants increase, some abundantly even rapaciously, so that it is wise to look the gift horse in the mouth. It may well be a winter heliotrope or a snow-in-summer disaster that is entering the garden gate.

Chapter 10

You Heave, I'll Grunt

Sometimes we have our noses too close to the ground. We ought to step back and view the whole from a more generous vantage point. Will you step back with me to the beginning of 'Observations of Modern Gardening, Illustrated by Descriptions,' printed for T. Payne at the Mews-gate London. My copy is the third edition of 1771.

'Gardening, in the perfection to which it has been lately brought in England, is entitled to a place of considerable rank among the liberal arts. It is as superior to landscape painting, as a reality to a representation; it is an exertion of fancy; a subject for taste; and being released now from the restraints of regularity, and enlarged beyond the purposes of domestic convenience, the most beautiful, the most simple, the most noble scenes of nature are all within its province; for it is no longer confined to the spots from which it borrows its name, but regulates also the disposition and embellishments of a park, a farm, or a riding; and the business of a gardener is to select and to apply whatever is great, elegant, or characteristic in any of them; to discover and to show all the advantages of the place upon which he is employed; to supply its defects, to correct its faults, and to improve its beauties. For all these operations, the objects of nature are still his only materials.

ROCK FRINGED GARDEN STEPS

His first enquiry, therefore, must be into the means by which those effects are attained in nature, which he is to produce, and into those properties in the objects of nature, which should determine him in the choice and arrangement of them.

'Nature, always simple, employs but four materials in the composition of her scenes, ground, wood, water, and rocks. The cultivation of nature has introduced a fifth species, the buildings requisite for the accommodation of men. Each of these again admits of varieties in figure, dimensions, colour, and situation. Every landscape is composed of these parts only; every beauty in a landscape depends on the application of their several varieties.'

Polish your spade, or, better still, borrow a bulldozer. Here we go.

Of Ground

The shape of ground must be either a convex, a concave, or a plane; in terms less technical called a swell, a hollow, and a level. By combinations of these are formed all the irregularities of which ground is capable; and the beauty of it depends on the degrees and the proportions in which they are blended.

'Both the convex and the concave are forms themselves of more variety, and may therefore be admitted to a greater extent than a plane; but levels are not totally inadmissible. The preference unjustly shown to them in the old gardens, where they prevailed almost in exclusion of every other form, has raised a prejudice against them. It is frequently reckoned an excellence in a piece of made ground, that every part of it is uneven; but

184

...iria Aquatica Variegata

Setting of foliage plants helps to liven up an otherwise dull corner

AQUATIC and BOG PLANTS

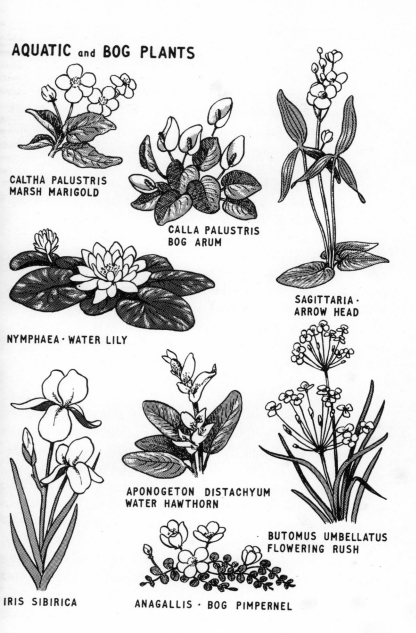

CALTHA PALUSTRIS
MARSH MARIGOLD

CALLA PALUSTRIS
BOG ARUM

SAGITTARIA ·
ARROW HEAD

NYMPHAEA · WATER LILY

APONOGETON DISTACHYUM
WATER HAWTHORN

BUTOMUS UMBELLATUS
FLOWERING RUSH

IRIS SIBIRICA

ANAGALLIS · BOG PIMPERNEL

then it wants one of the three great varieties of ground, whic
may sometimes be intermixed with the other two. A gentl
concave declivity falls and spreads easily on a flat; the channe
between several swells degenerate into mere gutters, if som
breadth be not given to the bottoms by flattening them; an
in many other instances, small portions of an inclined o
horizontal plane may be introduced into an irregular compos
tion. Care only must be taken to keep them down as subordina
parts, and not to suffer them to become principal.'

What a wonderful wide view of gardening they had. It
refreshing to read and the book is full of sound sense thoug
the viewpoint is so different from that of today's horticulturalist
Now we are in an age of specialists in horticulture as in all els
This man is the expert on mustard but that one is the leadir
authority on cress. The rock garden enthusiasts may b
interested in some of 'observations,'

Of Rocks

Rills, rivulets, and cascades, abound among rocks; they a
natural to the scene; and such scenes commonly require eve
accompaniment which can be procured for them: mere roc
unless they are peculiarly adapted to certain impressions, m
surprise, but can hardly please; they are too far removed fro
common life, too barren, and unhospitable; rather desolate th
solitary, and more horrid than terrible; so austere a charac
cannot be long engaging, if its rigour be not softened
circumstances, which may belong either to these or to mo
cultivated spots; and when the dreariness is extreme, lit

streams and waterfalls are of themselves insufficient for the purpose; an intermixture of vegetation is also necessary; and on some occasions even marks of inhabitants are proper.'

Gardening literature abounds with excellent plans for the daily, weekly and monthly work to be done in the garden. I have a suspicion that there is somewhere a family, like the Rothschilds of long standing, that early on cornered the market for 'gardening notes' and has since lived a life of elegant luxury in gardenless town houses. It is probably another branch of the same family that does all the 'Aunt Emily' columns. A relatively early example in the genre follows. It is quoted from 'The Instructor; or Young Man's Best Companion, to which is added The Family's Best Companion; and A Compendium of Geography and Astronomy, also some useful Interest-Tables; by George Fisher, Accountant published in Edinburgh. Printed Gavin Alston, Sold by P. Anderson, Bookseller Parliament Square. My edition is dated 1780. Probably December is one of the slackest months in the garden. This is what Mr. Fisher, accountant, suggests should be done.

DECEMBER
Pleasure Garden

'Draw the mats and cloths over the ranunculus and anemony-beds in fevere weather, whether froft or cold rains; but give them air in the middle of every tolerable day, and as foon as poffible uncover them all day; but draw on the mats aginft night.

Throw up the earth where flowering-frubs are to be planted n fring; and once in a fortnight turn it.

187

Dig up the borders that are to have flower-roots planted i
them in the fring, and give them the advantage of a fallow, b
throwing up the ground in a ridge.

Scatter over it a very little rotten dung from a melon-be
and after this turn it twice during the winter.

Look over the flowering-frubs, and prune them. Cut awa

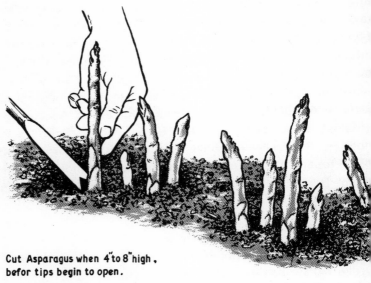

Cut Asparagus when 4" to 8" high,
befor tips begin to open.

all dead wood, fhorten luxuriant branches; and if any cr
each other, take away one. Leave them fo that the air can ha
free paffage between them.

Sift a quarter of an inch of good frefh mould over the roots
perennial-flowers whofe flalks have been cut down, and th

188

rake over the borders. This will give the whole an air of culture and good management, which is always pleasing.

Kitchen-garden

Plant cabbages and favoys for feed. This is to be done with great care; dig up a dry border, and break the mould very well; then take fome of the ftouteft cabbage and favoy plants; hang them up by the ftalkes five days, and then plant them half-way of the ftalk into the ground, draw up a good quantity of the mould about the part of the ftalk that is out of the ground, and make it into a kind of hill round each; then leave them to nature.

Sow another crop of peafe, and plant another parcel of beans, to take their chance for fucceeding the others.

Make another hot-bed for afparagus, to yield a fupply when the former is exhaufted. Continue to earth up celery, and cover fome endive with a good quantity of pea-ftraw, as it is growing, that you may take it up when wanted, which otherwife the froft will prevent.

Orchard and fruit-garden

Prepare for planting trees where they will be wanted in fring, by digging the ground deep, and turning it well now in the places where they are to ftand.

Scatter over the borders where the fruit-trees are planted fome frefh mould, and fome old dung, and in a mild day dig it in with a ftrong three pronged fork.

Look over the orchard trees, and cut away fuperfluous and

dead wood. Let the branches ftand clear of one another, tha
the air can get between; and the fruit will be better flavourec

This is the management of old trees, and new planted one
are to be preferved by covering the ground at their roots.

Instructions for marking on line; how to pickle and preferse
to make divers forts of wine of our Englifh product; togethe
with many excellent and approved medicines. falves, & neceffar
in all families.'

Sorry we seemed to have slipped into Mr. Foster's nex
section.

You will have recognised the genuine gardening note style
How many times have we all read that sentence beginning
'Look over the flowering shrubs. Cut away etc.' Again ther
is that point about a 'ftrong three pronged fork.' It is just th
sort of expertise that scares us and put us in awe of the exper
I feel sure someone must have seen me sally forth with a
ordinary four pronged one, slink back, clean it and start afres
as if for the first time with the genuine three pronged one. Yo
will have noted that Mr. Foster, like all gardening note writer
since, believes he is writing for a race of giants capable c
prodigous feats in the garden in between running to draw mat
over the anemony beds and hanging favoy plants upside dow
for five days.

It may well be that having made up another hot bed fe
afparagus and scattering a little rotten dung from a melon-be
you may feel a touch of ague coming on, Mr. Foster recommenc
the following. 'Drink the decoration (that is the boiling of ar
herb) of camomile, and fweeten it with treacle; which drir

190

when warm in bed, and fweat two hours. Or, to the wrifts apply a mixture of rune, muftard, and chinmey-foot, by way or plaifter.' I suggest that it is better to get a little of the gripes rather than ague and, 'Take a fliced nugmet in a quartern of brandy warmed over the fire; to which put the beaten yolk of an egg, with a little water or fugar; ftir them together over the fire to thicken a little; take it at night going to bed.' There is a useful recipe for the 'almonds of the ears fallen down.' But perhaps you can write me about this.

Mr. Fisher suggests the way towards giving the garden 'an air of culture and good management, which is always so pleasing.' But the matter is not so simple. The trouble is in the border and here we have the advice of 'A Head Gardener' writing in 'The Floral World and Garden Guide' on 'Bedders and Bedding, No III.'

'It is now, however, generally admitted, thanks to the teaching of our Editor here and elsewhere, that without the assistance of manure, in some form, flower gardening cannot be carried on successfully with any more success than would be attendant on an attempt to grow vegetables without maintaining the fertility of the soil by means of liberal dressings of fertilising matters. This point being conceded, all that need be said can be summed up in a very few words. First of all, it is necessary to decide upon the arrangements without delay, if not already done, to avoid delay and confusion at planting-time, and also to insure the beds being prepared in a manner most congenial to the subjects with which they are occupied during the ensuing season. The arrangements being determined upon, and the way in which each bed is to be planted duly entered in a book, the work of preparation must be proceeded with as fast as the beds are cleared of their winter occupants. All the beds should be dug up as deeply as it is possible to dig them; but if all receive an equal dressing of manure, the manure will be worse than wasted; because plants that do best in poor soil will grow too luxuriantly for them to flower well, whilst others that require a very liberal share of nourishment will be partially starved for the want of food. Bedding geraniums of all kinds with but few exceptions indeed, do much best when planted in newly manured ground, as also do centaureas, the dwarf tagetes and a few other things could be mentioned. On the other hand, violas, calceolarias, and verbenas seldom do well unless the ground has been liberally dressed with half-rotton manure. For such things as petunias, ageratums, heliotropiums and most of the ornamental leaved plants used for bedding, an intermediate course is desirable, so as to maintain a healthy and moderately vigorous growth without encouraging excessive luxuriance.'

What splendid urgency there is about the whole passage. No wonder the railways got built. What attention to detail. But we must guard against excessive luxuriance. Do we hear the Band of Hope in the background.

Elsewhere I have suggested that shrubs are the answer to many people's gardening problems. But sometimes a shrub presents a problem, it grows too well and overflows the space allocated to it. It needs moving. Perhaps you would like to invest in a 'Small Machine for Lifting Specimen Shrubs and

Conifers.' Perhaps they are the answer to your Christmas present problem. W. Robinson describes the machine in 'The Parks, Promenades, and Gardens of Paris' of 1869.

Transplanting Apparatus for Small Gardens

'Besides the above-described excellent method for the removal

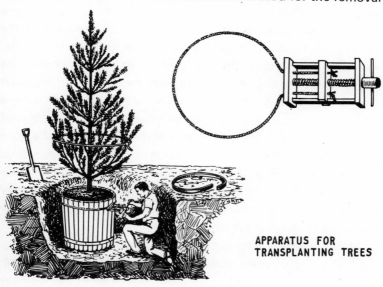

APPARATUS FOR
TRANSPLANTING TREES

of large trees, there is a very good method employed for the transplantation of small trees, specimen conifers, evergreens, and like subjects. Round each tree a circular trench is opened large enough for a man to move about in at his ease. The depth should be equal to that of the deepest large roots, and a ball of earth enough to insure the safe removal of the tree should

193

be left. All the smaller roots found in the trench should be carefully preserved. The ball is shaped into the form of a truncated cone, with its smallest portion below. It is next surrounded with light deal boards, separated from each other by the distance of three-quarters of an inch or so, like the staves of a barrel. They are next secured temporarily, by a suitable rope. A man descends into the hole and fixes the rope by means of the screw apparatus shown here, so as to press the planks firmly against the soil of the ball. The press is then removed and the same thing done higher up, within say four inches of the top, an ordinary cask hoop being first nailed round the planks before the screw is unfixed. The ball being firmly fixed in its proper position, it is hove over so as to get to its underneath part. The bottom of the cask having its boards fastened together with a circular piece of sheet iron rather larger than itself is passed under, the iron being pierced with two or three holes and turned up so that it may be nailed against the planks. In some cases the stem of the tree should be fixed by iron wire to the sides of the improvised cask.

'When it reaches its destination it is gently inclined to one side and the bottom boards removed. The hoops are next unfastened, the boards removed, and the roots carefully arranged in their natural position, some good earth being spread over them. The amount of success capable of being attained by this method may be seen throughout the squares of Paris, hardly a single tree having been killed during the plantation of the myriads now growing luxuriantly in that City.'

I enjoy reading clear instructions about any job. The great

Mr. Robinson's are as good as any. The bit that I particularly like is his thoughtfulness in ensuring that the trench around the shrub roots should be big enough for 'a man to move about in at his ease.' But even better is the characteristic horticultural pruned paragraph. Up to the cask having its bottom put on we are heaving and grunting along with Mr. Robinson. Then we read 'When it reaches its destination.' Mr. Robinson assumes the race of gardener-supermen, the whole cask with shrub being lifted from its hole and brought to its new home in a twinkling of an eyelid. Or perhaps every garden of those days had tackle for winching up and transporting shrubs in the garden shed alongside the three pronged fork. I do not know but there certainly were plenty of tools for pruning.

Nature had to be corrected and improved. The art of pruning was brought to wonderful heights in the last century. Charles Baltet's excellent treatise on 'Grafting and Budding' outlines some of the possibilities and methods. All is severely practical except for the opening quotation from Shakespeare,

> 'You see, sweet maid, we marry
> A gentle scion to the wildest stock;
> And make conceive a bark of baser kind
> By bud of nobler race; this is an art
> Which does mend nature; change it rather: but
> The art itself is nature.'

Perhaps you would like to mend nature along with M. Baltet.

Approach-Grafting in Figure-Training

'In order to show the happy results of grafting by approach,

195

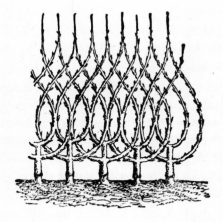

we have figured some specimens of espaliers trained in the garden of M. Nallet, at Brunoy. The trainer, M. Forest, has employed grafting either to complete their construction or to preserve the equilibrium of growth. MM. Van Hulle and Burvenich described these trees, in 1867, in their reports to the Belgian Government. Annexed is a representation of an espalier of pear-trees, formed with small palmettes, the branches of which interlace and touch each other. The trees are grafted at the points of contact, in the centre of the design, where the branches touch back to back, and not where they cross and diverge. The slight curvature of the branches which gives each tree an elliptical outline, is favourable to the development of fruiting branches; the extremities are inarched into the leading shoot formed by the union of the branches of the third series. The next illustration is a variety of the preceding arrangement, and a preferable one. It requires only palmettes of two series,

196

and the sinuous form of the branches permits long pruning, and maintains the fruit spurs regular. The leading shoots are crossed in lozenge form, and are grafted by approach at the top. This charming design, which is less complicated than it

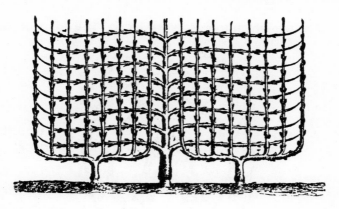

appears, is produced with regularity if the outline has been previously traced with switches fastened to the trellis. In the third illustration a palmette and two chandeliers are united and support each other mutually. The extremities of the branches of the horizontal palmette are inarched into the outer branches of the chandeliers. It is better not to graft the branches where they cross each other. A group like this should be grown in the open ground, and not against a wall. The figure represents a palmette—chandelier, of which the branches—following a regular curve, and grafted together at the ends—represent a target. In the centre, M. Forest has formed a letter by approach-grafting. A row of six such trees exhibits the name of M. Nallet.

197

In designs of this kind we prefer that the letters should take the most prominent part, and not be merely accessory; and thus we have formed the name of our establishment in one of our borders. Each pear tree forms one letter, so that in case of damage, the injury can be more speedily repaired than in the case of a tree which forms several letters. The different modes

of grafting by approach are useful here. A similar design has been formed with peach trees on a wall.'

The times they are a' changing

Perhaps we have laboured enough with the pruning knives outside. In the cold of the winter it is pleasant to come under glass in an artificial climate, perhaps similar to that suggested by James Barnes, in 'The Floral World and Garden Guide,' 1869

'The Cultivation of the Pineapple

In two chapters—No. 1.

By James Barnes,

Head Gardener to Lady Rolle, Bicton.

"Some young gardeners have an idea that we old pine-growers are stored with strange secrets, and when they see our well-finished pines on the exhibition table, a pang of envy sometimes possesses them, instead of a passion of emulation. I must be now one of the oldest pine-growers in the country, and if I testify that in the course of my time pine-growing has undergone great changes, it will be something towards dispelling the almost unpardonable notion, that there are secrets to be learnt, or that we who have led the way in improvement have any desire to carry with us our knowledge to the grave. No, no; I can call to mind the time when annual disrooting was practised, and shading was considered essential, and powerful stimulants were employed, in the hope thereby of counteracting the destructive practices that were prompted by ignorance, but which only added to the evil it was intended to remedy. Truly, the times change, and we change with them. But, my young friends, remember, plants do not change; the constitution of the pine is the same now as when it first came to these shores, and if we are to grow it, we must know something about that constitution and its requirements. When I have taken the principal prizes for finished pines, at such meetings as those at Regent's Park, my friends have pressed me to tell something of my practices, and I have said just what I say now to you. Success in pine-growing can only be accomplished by adapting the cultivation to the natural requirements of the plant. Well, you ask, what are those natural requirements, Well, read some good books of travel, or some trustworthy account of the products of the West Indies, and you will learn that the pine grows on sandy slopes, in the most intense sunshine that, perhaps, anywhere falls upon this bonny world. There, my young friend, is the key to your success, if you can see it." '

Mr. Barnes continues and gives his guidance for young pineapple growers in some considerable and interesting detail. They were giants these men, the head gardeners. Like the old cricketers they were a little bigger than life size. But of course in those days the number of vocations was more limited. A man would be pleased to come up out of the mine to play cricket for his county. He may today, but he has the opportunity of a thousand and one other well paid jobs with good pensions, expenses account, a car and status. But I wonder whether Mr. Barnes ever had the trouble that 'A Town Amateur' experienced. He writes in an issue not long after the Pineapple chapters.

'Cats, in Connection with the Gardenesque.

"Dreadful subject! how shall it be dealt with in a way to instruct and not offend? Not being by nature a cat-hater, it cannot be alleged of me that I have no feeling for the feline race; yet hatred of cats has become associated with thoughts of gardening, because of the persistent way the cats wage war against my out-door pleasures. Would the reader endure a categorical catalogue of my catastrophes—of glass smashed, plants torn up by the roots, of flower-beds desecrated by their nocturnal gambols, of blanks here, there, and everywhere, in addition to the blank on my face through the havoc of the grim grimalkins? I am so sure that it would be followed by catalepsy for me to tell the tale of a cat that plagued me this very week, that it is not likely I shall ever reveal the whole of my experience; indeed, I must already appear to be using catachrestical language, as if instead of an old tom mowking and mewing and caterwauling, he should put on spectacles and gravely talk Greek. No; fear not I will afflict you with my whole mind upon the subject, but just allow me to give you a few hints.

First as to glass houses, etc, etc. The first house I ever built had a nearly flat roof. It suited admirably both for the plants within and the cats without. The cats used to scamper over it quite easily, and now and then one would fall through and run about amongst my geraniums to find a place to get out again; and at last, made desperate with the prospect of permanent imprisonment, make a place of exit by smashing of a lot of glass. I one day saw a huge tom cat that I knew to be guilty of nibbling my carnations, and other feats of destructiveness, take up his seat peaceably in the sun on the edge of a frame in front of my low roofed greenhouse. Presently two or three more cats appeared on the top of the house together, like a little party assembling by agreement. The huge tom made a spring on to the roof, and joined them, and they commenced on my glass some extraordinary gambols. "This must be put a stop to," says I to myself, and I ran towards the house, threw up my hand,

and uttered the "sheesh," which people usually employ to scare cats away. They all bolted except one, and that was the very tom aforesaid, for as ill-luck would have it, he had thrust one of his legs through a hole in the glass, and began to struggle terribly to extricate it. In another moment he went clean through into the midst of my melons and geraniums. I had the good sense (it was a wonder I had any sense, so scared was I at what might happen) to run instantly and open the door. Confound him! instead of seeing that escape was easy, he commenced leaping frantically in order to get out the same way that he came in. Up and down, up and down he went, as if madness had seized him. Every time he leaped he smashed the glass with his head; every time he came down the glass rattled about him, and terrified him more. Oh, it was an awful scene! I went along the front of the house, and looked down into it in order to frighten him out, but he was too bewildered either to see me making faces at him from without, or the door standing open for his escape. Presently he made another leap under my very eyes, and I felt the splinters of glass run fast in my face, and next instant saw him run through the whole body of plants that stood on the front stage, scattering them on all sides, and joy! joy! he bolted out and was gone! There was a track of blood in the course he pursued, and that is all I know as to the extent of his sufferings, for I never saw him again. Now, strange to say, I do not know what is the maximum of slope which a cat can run upon; if I did, a rule might be given to the effect— never have the roof of a greenhouse below an angle of—. It strikes me that a roof at forty-five degrees would be too steep for cats; however, I have mine always sharper than 45°. Never while I live in town, will I again build a greenhouse or a pit with a roof over which cats can perambulate. If I must have a nearly flat roof, I will protect it with wire netting, and surround it with palisades of spikes. They shall be tickled in the toes as badly as if put upon hot bricks ere they shall enjoy a war-dance on my glass again.

'Cats make runs, and appear to give preference to the best flowerbeds and borders for this purpose. When I find an alley cut through my plants by cats rushing along at night, I put in a lot of small sharp sticks aslant, all manner of ways. Next night as they make a rush, their tender noses strike the pointed sticks, and they howl and run away. It has long been a rule with me to surround any plant I am very choice about with sticks put in aslant; it is a golden preventive of destruction. Another means of keeping the place clear is to keep a sharp dog always loose, and train him to respect your plants. This may be done most easily; my dog never steps across the box edging, or quits the proper path under any circumstances. Now and then, perhaps, the dog may give chase, and make a splendid run amongst a lot of roses or verbenas, and cause you to doubt if this preventive is not as bad as the disease. But in the end, if the dog is kept in good training, the place will be pretty safe against cats, for they do not care to meet a dog that has a penchant for hunting them; and, after all, a bad dog will never do so much harm in a garden as the dozens of cats that might infest it were the dog not there. Yet one more hint to lovers of flowers who are plagued by cats. Suppose you have a bed of geraniums or of carnations as I could show you now; the cats might assemble and have a scrimmage in the midst of it, and scatter the plants all over the place in the form of mincemeat any night in the season. I render such a misfortune impossible. First, I enclose the bed with a neat wire fence six inches high: though a cat would jump this easy enough, nevertheless, it is very likely no cat will. But before I plant the bed I stretch stout copper wire across it in five or six directions making the wire fast to the boundary fence. I used to lose a whole bed of pinks before adopting these measures, but have not lost one since. Probably the fence keeps them off, and the wire is not wanted. Certainly a bed on grass looks exceedingly neat and finished with only these low wire fences, so there is no wrong done to the gardenesque by the procedure. Well, there is one more mode of action, that of banishment, to be practised as follows:-

'(This, the concluding paragraph of the essay, must not appear; we could not mar the pages of the Floral World by giving publicity to our correspondent's system of poisoning cats. Supposing, even, that indiscriminate killing of these animals were allowable (and of course it is not allowable, on ground no less of common honesty than of humanity), the practice of placing poison within their reach might oftentimes lead to consequences of the most serious nature, such as every one of our readers will, on the instant, apprehend. Ed. F. W.))

The cats, like the gardeners, seem to have been bigger in those days.

Past gardening books and many present ones delight in giving in every muscle-tearing detail on how a portion of ground should be properly trenched. The best instructions give diagrams neatly marked with volumes of soil marked A, B, C, D etc. To start with, that marked A has to be placed on top of that marked B, and so on. I do not quote any passage at length as, not only is there the danger that the casual glancer through this book may think he has picked on a treatise about methods of archaeological excavation or an account of trench warfare in the Great War, there is the memory of long days trenching not the kitchen garden, or a portion, but whole fields. A was moved to B and C to D. E was dug. F was frosted. G was returned to H, and I was tired, very tired at the end of each long day. I suppose it did our souls good, I cannot think it did all that was claimed for it in the books. The soil that the Good Lord put umpteen feet underground was put there for a purpose, not for us to go playing about with.

Let us leave the trenching awhile and mow the lawn. A good lawn is something both soothing and pleasing to the eye. We can ask for advice, perhaps like the American visitor who was answered, 'How did we get the grass so nice. Well, it's simple. We just mowed it and rolled it for three hundred years.' Or we can read Clare Leighton in 'Four Hedges,' 1935. 'How many people know the right way it should be done? Feet should be bare; grass should be slightly damp. The cold, moist clover strikes up from the mower upon my bare feet, and blades of cut grass and bits of slashed weeds stick between my toes.'

I think we might leave the lawn too. Let us settle in our armchairs and look at some catalogues. Perhaps we can bear in mind the advice of Gertrude Jekyll in 'Home and Garden' 1900.

'Now that there is so much to choose from, we should not let any mental slothfulness stand in the way of thinking and watching and comparing, so as to arrive at a just appreciation of its merits and uses of all our garden plants.

'It is not possible to use to good effect all the plants that are to be had. In my own case I should wish to grow many more than just those I have, but if I do not find a place where my critical garden conscience approves of having any one plant I would rather be without it. It is better to me to deny myself the pleasure of having it, than to endure the mild sense of guilt of having placed it where it neither does itself justice nor accords with its neighbours, and where it reproaches me every time I pass it.' Even sterner warnings come from Osbert Sitwell in 'Penny Foolish,' 1935.

'Flowers, I have written, should be confined to a flower-garden; but, even there, they should form only the borders to long, rolling waves of sea-green cabbages and be interspersed with the purple pom-poms of the artichoke, with the knobs of onions and the scarlet flowers of the bean. They should be edged, too, with fruit trees. There should be myrtle, verbena and bay trees, and, above all, no attempt at a daring herbaceous border.

'Moreover, the few flowers you have, should be very specially chosen, selected for their beauty in dying and in death as much for their beauty in the full unfolding of life; that is to say, one should be as much influenced by their habits of growth as by their blossom. For what is life, except a long process—varying individually, it is true, in its length—of death? And just as the

206

Greeks used to maintain that no man could be happy or fortunate until he was dead, so can no flower be considered beautiful until it is fallen. Thus the Chinese, most wise and subtle race, allow the quality of beauty to no flower which does not maintain an exquisite form and colour in its decay.'

Catalogues make good reading, often entertaining and informative, though perhaps on occasion not exactly the revealed truth. Catalogues vary in value, phraseology, and truthfulness. I believe they are now rather better than they have been in the past. But the tyro finding his way through some brightly coloured tome may find himself floundering among the adjectives. The following is given as a very rough introduction to a subject that is too vast to be dealt with here in any but a very cursory way. The greatest difficulty in defining terms commonly appearing in catalogues is that a word in one catalogue may be given different weight and value than the same one in another. An example of this is,

Novelty. In the pages of the specialists this may mean, a plant introduced into commerce the current year. In other more general catalogues the term may define a plant that is newer than the other varieties listed under one species of plant. In at least one current catalogue the term is used to describe three plants all of which entered commerce before the First World War. Of course from the wider viewpoint, remembering the Romans possibly introduced Walnuts, Spanish Chestnuts, Sycamores and other plants, these three novelties are, relatively speaking, new, but it seems to stretch the usually accepted meaning of the word a trifle.

Top size. Used for referring to plants for sale, especially in bulbs tubers, rhizomes and other nobbly kinds. It is taken as axiomatic that all other sizes having been sold, that which remains shall be termed 'Top size.'

Recommended. A very good stock of this is held by the catalogue compiler.

Recommended for mass planting. The stock of this variety is smothering the nursery and is getting through the hedges.

Medium sized. Used often to refer to flower size. Means small.

Striking. Is marked or twisted in such a manner as to make one wonder whether it is virus induced or whether some other agency should be looked for.

Sensation. Used as in, 'This was a sensation at the C———a Show.' It is not often thought necessary to include the date of the show. It means, more than one person mentioned the variety to the salesman. This is slightly heavier currency than 'recommended.'

Sturdy. This is a word often used about flowers commonly grown in the garden but also for cutting such as daffodils or tulips. It means the stems are about two or three inches long.

Never fails to attract attention. The nurseryman going through his nursery has his attention attracted to this variety. It can mean, 'Why on earth did we spend so much time propagating this thing.'

Indispensable. At one time a favourite adjective for alpines. Means commonly grown, dispensable.

Choice. This can be used in a variety of ways. The commonest use of the word means, will probably die within six months.

Useful. Curiously this word crops up in very many catalogues of all types and of all levels of trustworthyness. It probably does not need any explanation. It is usually used barely but can be tied in a phrase in this manner, useful for cutting, useful for forcing. If the nurseryman is forced back on the word useful, it surely means that the variety is one that is unlikely to repel or indeed to be noticed at all. 'Comely' or 'homely' are possibly from the same vein of adjectives applied in another field.

Mixed. That which is left when all other orders have been met. Usually means more than one sort though this is not guaranteed. One nurseryman friend bought a quarter of a ton of mixed daffodils and narcissi to brighten up his shrub nursery. They all opened the same day, thousands upon thousands of Narcissus 'Flower Record' nodded their heads at him in sprightly dance or something or other.

Needs some protection. Will die at first hint of frost.

Decorative. A term used in describing a variety of flowers often used in exhibition. (Excluding the specialist use of it in describing a class of dahlias). It means, quite useless for exhibition, with petals twisted like a corkscrew when they should be flat or alternatively flat as a pane of glass when they should be twisted like a corkscrew.

Very vigorous, Useful for rough parts, Will naturalise. Varies from catalogue to catalogue in meaning, but may often be taken to read, an invasive rampant weed which it is better to allow the Coal Board to experiment with on their black alps than to allow in one's own plot.

disease resistant. May not be very startling but at least has not died in the nursery.

*These asterisks are used for a variety of purposes. Sometimes they merely mean that the varieties have a scent. If used for recommending special varieties will mean something like the following interpretation.

　　*=stock of say 1,000 plants.　　**=stock of 10,000 plants.
=stock of 100,000 plants.　　*=stock of 1,000,000 plants.

Gardening books may help one make a choice of things to plant. The famous quote from Beverley Nichols, 'Down the Garden Path,' 1932, reminds one to be careful. 'If you want to begin with something that is quite foolproof, you cannot do better than invest in a few roots of *Petasites fragrans* which has the pretty English name of winter heliotrope.' The two biggest colonies I know of this foolproof plant both happen to be in graveyards. It possibly just happens to be so. I do not suppose there is any significance in the fact. Maybe of course the winter heliotrope has always been there and no other use of the land seemed practicable. Winter heliotrope grows in the same delicate and hardy way as Colt's Foot, Ground Elder and Mare's tail. Such pretty names.'

END

Miniature Geraniums

Harold Bagust

This is the first book on Miniature Geraniums, and it is written by one of the country's leading experts.

It has been prepared from the experience of a lifetime's work on these plants and shows in great detail how these charming plants can be grown to perfection.

It also provides an up-to-date list of varieties and suppliers and has many line drawings plus colour photographs. It is a book which no true lover of Geraniums can be without.

100 *pages,* 15 *colour plates, many line drawings,* 12s.6d.

Mushroom Growing

Arthur Simons

Several years ago Arthur Simons wrote a book for those people who were interested in growing their own mushrooms. This book proved a best-seller for many years and became a classic on its subject. A few years ago that edition went out-of-print and it is because of unusually high public interest that it has now been reproduced in its entirety in an attractive paperback presentation.

For the many who are prepared to learn the simple methods of home cultivation this informative little book will prove invaluable and is destined for a long life of popularity.

96 *pages, line drawings,* 5s.

Clematis

Stanley B. Whitehead, D.Sc.

Climbers are among the most attractive and decorative of all plants. They can be trained up a wall, they can cover unsightly objects. Ugly things can be decorated in such a way that they become pleasing. Climbers can be shaped on almost any frame or support, and it is this pliancy that makes them so versatile. The author gives wide-ranging advice on growing all kinds of climbers and wall-shrubs: those we know and the rare things we've always wanted to grow but did not know how to set about it.

$8\frac{3}{4} \times 5\frac{1}{2}$ *in., 176 pages, monochrome and colour illustrations, 25s.*

Chrysanthemum Growing

H. G. Witham Fogg

Chrysanthemums are among the most popular of all garden and greenhouse flowers. The author is well known as a writer on gardening matters and this book bears the stamp of one who really knows his subject. It is essentially a book for the practical gardener, but this does not bar it from a casual or week-end enthusiast. Propagation and general cultivation are fully covered and there is valuable information regarding marketing. Operations such as timing and stopping, which sometimes seem so involved, are explained in simple language. The author gives interesting information and advice on the origins, types, and exhibiting of Chrysanthemums, and this straightforward guide is a book that every garden lover will treasure.

$8 \times 5\frac{1}{4}$ *in., 190 pages, monochrome and colour illustrations, 25s.*

Climbing Plants and some Wall Shrubs

Douglas Bartrum

Climbing plants are now accepted as part of modern house and garden decoration but many who wish to incorporate plants in their interior or garden design are not gardeners and do not feel able to go ahead with their plans without some guidance. A guide is the true description of this book, for Mr. Bartrum does not write for the experienced botanist but rather for the casual gardener who needs expert help to get good results. All aspects of cultivating climbers is carefully described and the wide range of types and colours is fully explained. With this book even the person whose gardening experience is restricted to window boxes, can achieve excellent results and surprise himself with the versatility of the plant he has grown.

$8\frac{3}{4} \times 5\frac{1}{2}$ in., 204 pages, colour and monochrome illustrations, 25s.

Water in the Garden

Douglas Bartrum

This book shows how to use water to the best effect in the garden. It shows how formal and informal pools and ponds may be built. It describes the use of fountains and streams and with its guidance the enthusiastic handyman can build a pool to be proud of. Water is part of modern garden design and this guide makes its installation possible to the average handyman.

$8\frac{3}{4} \times 5\frac{1}{2}$ in., 192 pages, monochrome and colour illustrations, 25s.

Evergreens for your Garden

Douglas Bartrum

There are comparatively few books on Evergreens. This is an excellently produced volume which will have a strong appeal to gardeners and will be of inestimable value both to those who are planning a new garden and those who are on the look-out for labour-saving plants. (The dictum that "evergreens will smother your weeds" is famous in the gardening world.) Mr. Douglas Bartrum has produced a delightful and practical book, using non-technical language but including much technical information and many useful facts. The book is well illustrated with photographs and line drawings, the latter showing the structure of various types of evergreen leaves, etc., and also methods of propagating evergreen plants, which are often expensive to buy. This book has much to offer anyone with a general interest in gardening.

$8\frac{3}{4} \times 5\frac{1}{2}$ *in., 194 pages, monochrome and colour illustrations, 25s.*

Begonias, Gloxinias and African Violets

H. G. Witham Fogg

Here is a complete guide for the beginner, and also one which will be of help to experienced growers of these three lovely subjects.

Whether you want to grow begonias in the greenhouse, living room, or the garden—or if you want to try your hand at exhibiting—this book will prove invaluable.

There is not much literature on gloxinias, and here, the author gives us all we need to know regarding the history, cultivation and propagation of these intriguing plants.

The *Saintpaulia* or African Violet is a fashionable plant and it is not really difficult to cultivate. The author shows how African Violets can be had in bloom for many months, by recognizing and supplying their needs.

$8\frac{3}{4} \times 5\frac{1}{2}$ *in., 175 pages, monochrome and colour illustrations. 25s.*

Success with Shrubs and Trees

Fred W. Loads

In recent years the value of trees and shrubs, as both labour-saving and attractive residents of any garden, has become increasingly evident.

This book covers all that one needs to know in order to grow the recommended varieties successfully. Not forgotten are such problems of modern living such as screening manhole covers, oil storage tanks, and ugly garages and sheds.

$8\frac{3}{4} \times 5\frac{1}{2}$ *in.*, 188 *pages*, 28 *photos*, 25s.

Geraniums and Pelargoniums

H. G. Witham Fogg

In this book the author deals fully with all aspects of the culture of these most popular flowering and ornamental plants. There are chapters on culture, propagation, winter care, pests and diseases. We are shown how geraniums can be used for window boxes, tubs and baskets, how to select plants wisely, and grow geraniums in the garden and greenhouse.

$8\frac{3}{4} \times 5\frac{1}{2}$ *in.*, 156 *pages*, 4 *colour plates*, 34 *photos*, 21s.

Daffodils, Tulips and other Hardy Bulbs

Michael Jefferson-Brown

Of all garden subjects, the hardy bulb is perhaps the one which, more than any other, combines ease of cultivation with a truly rewarding display of colour and elegance—and that at a time when the garden is only just beginning to throw off the shackles of winter. Like many other "easy" subjects, however, that little extra care in preparation, understanding of requirements, and cultivation brings great dividends. Michael Jefferson-Brown explains in this practical and comprehensive book how every gardener can obtain the best possible results from daffodils, tulips, crocuses and the many other delightful hardy bulbs.

The author is one of our leading growers of flowers from bulbs, and his wide experience makes this book a real investment for all garden lovers.

$8\frac{3}{4} \times 5\frac{1}{2}$ *in.*, 160 *pages*, *monochrome illustrations/line drawings*, 25s.

All About Greenhouses
A. J. Simons

Many books have been written to instruct the private gardener in the art of growing greenhouse plants, but this is the only book which seeks to guide the amateur to the purchase of the right greenhouse in the first place and tells him how to heat and equip it to meet his particular requirements. There are now so many different types of greenhouse on the market and so many different ways of heating them that far too many beginners make an ill-advised purchase to begin with, underestimate the cost of heating and finally suffer disappointment through their failure to obtain the results they had hoped for. Such disappointments can be avoided if they read this book.

$8\frac{3}{4} \times 5\frac{1}{2}$ *in.*, 224 *pages, monochrome illustrations and line drawings,* 25s.

Gardening with Cloches
Louis N. Flawn

Here is a book devoted entirely to up-to-date methods of cloche gardening. It helps the gardener to select cloches, to set them out on the best site and advises him on the problems of soil preparation and growing the crops.

It is written in the simple, straight forward style that makes Mr. Flawn's books and articles so popular with the gardening public. He is not only an enthusiast on cloche cultivation, but has unrivalled experience of his subject and yet understands the problems that confront the novice.

It is a book that will help the gardener to get the best from his cloches, and one which he will need for reference throughout the year.

$8\frac{3}{4} \times 5\frac{1}{2}$ *in.*, 208 *pages, monochrome and colour illustrations,* 21s.

The Cool Greenhouse all the Year Round
Louis N. Flawn and V. L. Flawn, N.D.H.

It is not often that father and son co-operate in writing a book but here are two practical gardeners who have succeeded in producing a volume that will make strong appeal to keen gardeners. The book forms a guide to the successful cultivation of plants in a greenhouse of modest size in which a moderate temperature can be maintained—a typical house for the enthusiastic amateur. The emphasis is on the cultivation of plants that can be grown under cool conditions throughout the year rather than on those exotic greenhouse plants which are often beyond the scope and facilities of the average amateur.

This is a book that all greenhouse enthusiasts should have on their shelves.

$8\frac{3}{4} \times 5\frac{1}{2}$ *in.*, 162 *pages, monochrome illustrations and line drawings,* 21s.